DEDICATION

To the love of my life, my wife and soul mate Rhonda. What would life be like without you? Every day with you is a gift. Boy, did I marry over my head!

To my children, Rachel and Andrew. May you continue to grow in the wisdom of God. I love you!

To my mom, who taught me to live life in the moment.

To Keith Wasserman, one of the wisest persons I know. Thanks for our lifelong friendship.

ACKNOWLEDGMENTS

To Tom Walsh and the Maxwells' kindness for allowing me to use their condo in Florida to write this project.

To my soul brothers Larry Wagner and Hule Goddard. Thanks for the weekly times of prayer, laughter, sharing, and cinnamon crunch bagels.

SPECIAL THANKS TO MY RESEARCH TEAM

To my writing and research team, graduates of Columbia International University in Columbia, SC. Nick Cunningham, Trevor Miller, Anne Lord Bailey, and Rachel Olshine; and Kaisi Cunningham, a graduate of Asbury Seminary. Thanks for your diligent work and great insight.

CONTENTS

INTRODUCTION

How to Use *Studies on the Go*

Studies on the Go have all of the best ingredients for helping students and adults connect with God and each other as they encounter Scripture. These studies work best in a small group, but can also be utilized in Bible studies, Sunday school, or youth group or even on road trips and retreats.

Each session is broken up into the following subsections:

1. **Leader's Insight**: A brief overview for each lesson to help the leader/facilitator understand the historical background, focus, and purpose of the text.

2. **Share (warm-up questions):** Before jumping in and studying the Bible, it helps to allow time for your group to connect relationally first. Warm-up questions are lighter and help your group get comfortable interacting with one another.

3. **Observe (observation questions):** These questions help your group—regardless of their Bible knowledge—focus on "What does the passage say?" and "What is the author communicating?" The goal is to bring to the surface what the students are noticing about the passage.

4. **Think (interpretation questions):** These are a set of questions helping your group consider what the author meant when he wrote the letters. The goal is to discover what the writer was saying to his audience.

5. **Apply (application questions):** These questions are focused on helping the group connect God's truth to their own lives.

6. **Do:** An additional activity option that helps students experientially "flesh" out the lesson. The goal here is action, putting head knowledge into real-life practice.

7. **Quiet Time Reflections:** One reproducible handout page for each session providing additional exercises to help students personally reflect on the passages on a daily basis.

My hope is that these studies create an environment where students and adults experience community. The leader's job is to facilitate a safe place in which people can be known and share freely. The best small groups are fluid, organized, free-flowing—with each person sharing.

May God bless you as you engage students in the process of applying God's truth to their lives.

Blessings,

Dr. David Olshine

BACKGROUND INSIGHTS FOR PROVERBS

WHO? Most scholars believe King Solomon compiled these sayings known as Proverbs. Solomon loved knowledge as a young person (1 Kings 3:9-12). Bill T. Arnold and Bryan E. Beyer's *Encountering the Old Testament* refers to Solomon's status as a world leader, a brilliant and discerning man (Grand Rapids, MI: Baker Academic, 1999). He had vast interests in politics, science, business, and spiritual issues (see also 1 Kings 4:29-31).

WHAT? Proverbs are short, pithy sayings that provoke a response. They're practical in nature and teach lessons about life. The Book of Proverbs is a call to experience wisdom. Wisdom is personified in the form of a woman calling out to us, mocking the person who doesn't listen to her, because to resist wisdom leads often to poor choices. The Jewish perspective is that all of wisdom is wrapped up in "who God is" and that this God can be known and personally experienced.

Wisdom from the Proverbs calls us to a vertical dimension, relating to God through prayer and solitude. The Proverbs also call us toward wisdom in the horizontal issues of life: Child rearing, fearing God, helping the oppressed, responding to the poor, and counseling others. When we choose to live selfishly, Proverbs calls this foolishness; when we choose to live God's way, we experience wisdom.

WHY? The Proverbs were written in a simple way so readers would experience wisdom, discernment, justice, learning, and guidance. "Wisdom" is mentioned over 40 times in the book of Proverbs. Chapter 1 is a call to listen and apply wisdom.

WHERE? Proverbs follows the book of Psalms written by King David. The Psalter (another name for Psalms) is a collection of poems and wrenching cries from the heart. King David sets the stage for Solomon's writings by saying in Psalm 49:4, "I will turn my ear to a proverb." Ecclesiastes is the book following Proverbs, also written by King Solomon. Ecclesiastes is only 12 chapters, and Solomon's thesis is simple: Life without God at the core of our being is meaningless and empty. The finale of Solomon's trilogy follows Ecclesiastes in the Song of Songs. These are love songs and poetry between a man and a woman that mirror God's love for his people. These three books are rooted in Solomon's desire to communicate to us how to live life to the fullest.

SECTION ONE

1. BABY STEPS
Proverbs 1

LEADER'S INSIGHT

King Solomon was one of the wisest men ever to walk this planet. He penned these sayings, called "proverbs." The main theme throughout the 31 chapters is obtaining wisdom—but not just any wisdom. Proverbs is about a specific kind of wisdom: God's wisdom.

Proverbs doesn't refer to wisdom as information gathering; rather Proverbs talks about gaining God's information, called wisdom, which leads to transformation. In the same way a caterpillar morphs into a new species of being in the butterfly, when we allow God's wisdom to shape our thoughts and actions, we become different from those around us.

Author Eugene Peterson says in his introduction to Proverbs in his Bible translation THE MESSAGE, "Wisdom is the art of living skillfully in whatever actual conditions we find ourselves" (Colorado Springs, CO: NavPress, 2002). The book of Proverbs teaches us how to live skillfully. We desperately need wisdom for handling money, resolving conflict, taming our tongues, honoring our parents, loving the needy, checking our attitudes, and knowing what to do when faced with temptations and evil.

Knowledge is not enough; we need wisdom—God's wisdom. In Chapter 1 we'll explore how to get right with God and live skillfully according to God's wisdom. Proverbs 1:7 is one of the best-known texts in all of the Bible: "The fear of the Lord is the beginning of knowledge, but fools despise wisdom and instruction." To experience this kind of life successfully, we need to begin as most children do—taking baby steps. Let's dig in.

SHARE

- If you had 24 hours to spend with anyone, past or present, whom you consider full of wisdom, who would that person be?

- What's one of the dumbest or most embarrassing things you've ever done?

- What's something you wish you'd known a year ago that you know today?

OBSERVE

- Read Proverbs 1:1-7. What was Solomon's explanation of the purpose of his book? Based on verse 7, why should we "fear the Lord"? What does it mean to "fear the Lord"?

- Look at verses 8-19. What are some of the warnings listed? What did Solomon plead for in verse 15?

- In verses 20-27 what was the writer saying about wisdom's rebuke?

- Read verses 28-33. What's the result of rejecting God's wisdom?

THINK

- Based on verses 1-7, why is wisdom such a big deal? What are some ways to gain wisdom mentioned in these passages?

- Look at verses 8-10. What does listening to fathers' and mothers' instructions have to do with God's wisdom?

- Read verses 29-33. From these verses, how might you move closer to God? Away from God?

APPLY

•Which is harder—being corrected by a friend or by a parent? Why? Explain.

•Do you tend to listen to your parents' instructions or resist their advice?

•Are you a better listener or advice giver?

•How open are you to being corrected by someone on a scale of 1 (no way) to 10 (absolutely)?

DO

Watch the opening scene of the movie *What About Bob?* (1991) when Bob (Bill Murray) is in the office with his psychiatrist, Dr. Leo Marvin (Richard Dreyfuss). Bob hears the explanation of Marvin's new book, *Baby Steps,* and then proceeds to practice walking in and out of the office. After the clip have the students discuss the process of taking baby steps on becoming wiser. Then allow a debriefing time for students to complete this statement: "This week one baby step I will take toward seeking and applying God's wisdom to my life is [BLANK]." Have them write their ideas down (things stick better when we jot them on paper). Follow up on this next week; ask students to share what steps they took.

QUIET TIME REFLECTIONS

Day one: Proverbs 1:1-7

1. What word or phrase jumps out to you? Why?

2. Do you view yourself as a person of wisdom? Why or why not?

3. Think about the word *wisdom*. What does it mean for your life?

Day two: Proverbs 1:8-15

1. What word or phrase jumps out to you? Why?

2. What advice is given to overcome temptation?

3. Which temptations are you most vulnerable to give in to? Which ones are you most able to overcome?

Day three: Proverbs 1:16-19

1. What word or phrase jumps out to you? Why?

2. What do you think about the phrase "how useless to spread a net where every bird can see it"? What does this mean?

3. What are some ways to handle temptation?

Day four: Proverbs 1:20-22

1. What word or phrase jumps out to you? Why?

2. What's your response to handling correction?

3. What are practical ways you can be a teachable person?

Day five: Proverbs 1:23-27

1. What word or phrase jumps out to you? Why?

2. Does wisdom help us avoid bad choices, based on verses 26-27?

3. Think about the consequences of listening and learning. How does this impact the outcome of many situations?

Day six: Proverbs 1:28-33

1. What word or phrase jumps out to you? Why?

2. What does it mean that "they will eat the fruit of their ways" in verse 31?

3. How does God intend for us to make wise decisions?

Day seven: Proverbs 1:1-33

Read through the entire passage. Write down the one verse that impacted you the most this week. Commit the passage to memory.

2. FINDING THE GOOD TRAILS
Proverbs 2

LEADER'S INSIGHT

Walking in the woods is a refreshing experience. Most woods have many trails to walk. Some lead us to a certain destination, and others lead us into being lost. I enjoy hiking, especially when the trail is marked well (I don't really like bears or snakes). Proverbs 2 tells us about finding the good trails that lead toward wisdom.

The Bible speaks of many who were considered wise: Joshua (Deuteronomy 34:9), Abigail (1 Samuel 25:3), King David (2 Samuel 14:20), Daniel (Daniel 5:11-12), Jesus (Luke 2:52), Moses (Acts 7:20-22), and the Apostle Paul (2 Peter 3:15-16). These people had to make choices every day just as we do. The primary writer of Proverbs was King Solomon, who was considered the wisest of all by some and wiser than all the wisdom of Egypt (1 Kings 4:29-34).

Solomon desired wisdom more than wealth or stature, so God said, "I will give you a wise and discerning heart, so that there will never have been anyone like you" (1 Kings 3:12).

Proverbs 2:8-11 says—

> He keeps his eye on all who live honestly, and pays special attention to his loyally committed ones. So now you can pick out what's true and fair, find all the good trails! Lady Wisdom will be your close friend, and Brother Knowledge your pleasant companion. Good Sense will scout ahead for danger, Insight will keep an eye out for you. (MSG)

In this lesson your students will discover the trails to avoid because they lead us to destruction and the trails to take to obtain wisdom from God.

SHARE

•Name a time and situation in which you got lost.

•If you could visit any place but only travel by foot once you arrived there, where would that be and why?

•If you were given a compass, could you find your way around? Why or why not?

OBSERVE

•According to Proverbs 2:1-9 what seems to be the right path toward wisdom?

•Read verses 10-14. How will wisdom protect us?

•According to verses 15-19, what are some trails that will lead us off the wisdom path?

•Read verses 20-22. What happens to the upright and the wicked? (Also look up Psalm 37:9, 29, 38 and Proverbs 10:30).

THINK

•Why do you think the ear (verse 2) has anything to do with obtaining wisdom, fearing God, and knowing God (verse 5)?

•Read verse 11. What is discretion and how can it protect you?

•Look at verses 12-13. How can men whose "words are perverse, who have left the straight paths" have any influence on our walk with God?

APPLY

- When it comes to having an open heart and attentive ears to God, are you: (a) usually hit and miss, (b) pretty consistent, (c) striking out constantly, or (d) someone whose ears are so closed, you have no interest?

- Have you ever experienced crying "aloud for understanding, look[ing] for it as silver, and search[ing] for it as for hidden treasure" (verses 3-4)? Have you searched for wisdom and understanding from God? From others?

- Verses 16-20 describe the lure of a seductive woman. How can our sexual desires lead us down the wrong path? How is that path destructive?

- What are some of the paths you need to walk down to experience God's wisdom?

DO

Pick up the game Jenga (someone in your group probably has it). The object is to remove one block at a time and stack it on top of the pile. The last player to stack a block without the tower falling wins. It's a game of eye coordination, decision making, and wisdom. Play it as a group.

QUIET TIME REFLECTIONS

Day one: Proverbs 2:1-5

   1. What word or phrase jumps out to you? Why?

   2. What are some ways to experience the fear of God?

   3. How have you experienced God?How can you experience more of God?

Day two: Proverbs 2:6-11

   1. What word or phrase jumps out to you? Why?

   2. How can wisdom make people blameless?

   3. How can God give you wisdom to know right from wrong?

Day three: Proverbs 2:12-15

   1. What word or phrase jumps out to you? Why?

   2. What are some ways wisdom can save us?

   3. Do you reject or desire wisdom? Why?

Day four: Proverbs 2:16-18

   1. What word or phrase jumps out to you? Why?

   2. How can you avoid seductive situations?

   3. How can sexuality lead people toward God or away from God?

Day five: Proverbs 2:19-20

1. What word or phrase jumps out to you? Why?

2. What are some of the consequences of going down the wrong trail?

3. What are some of the things that keep you on the right trail?

Day six: Proverbs 2:21-22

1. What word or phrase jumps out to you? Why?

2. What are the implications of the wicked's and the upright's decisions?

3. How have you changed over the past two years?

Day seven: Proverbs 2:1-22

Read through the entire passage. Write down the one verse that impacted you the most this week. Commit the passage to memory.

3. WORDS TO KNOW-IT-ALLS
Proverbs 3

LEADER'S INSIGHT

Trust. What does this word mean to you? Not only is trust a difficult thing to receive, but it's also a difficult thing to give. How do we know whom to trust? Why should we trust them? Whom should I trust to give me direction concerning how I live my life?

Why do we have trouble trusting God? Trusting parents, friends, or someone we want to know more deeply? Could it be pride? Or maybe it's an issue of control. When we start thinking we know everything, we run into difficulty. Developing a know-it-all mentality is really dangerous, yet which of us hasn't been there, done it? Proverbs 3:7 tells it straight: "Don't assume that you know it all. Run to God! Run from evil!" (MSG)

The author assures us God is trustworthy for guidance and provision. Encourage your students to memorize Proverbs 3:5-6: "Trust in the Lord with all your heart and lean not on your own understanding; in all your ways submit to him, and he will make your paths straight."

God's wisdom is older than time itself. His wisdom isn't just a good idea, but it's the truth about why things are the way they are. We can be sure the wisdom God offers us will lead us into life abundantly, the way it was meant to be lived. And that might keep us from becoming know-it-alls.

SHARE

- What's the first thing you do when you find yourself in trouble?

- Have you ever tried to fix a big problem on your own and ended up just making it worse? Explain.

- Who's someone in your school, neighborhood, or church you think is a wise person? What do you think makes him wise?

OBSERVE

- Based on Proverbs 3:1-2, what will remembering this teaching do for you?

- Based on verses 5-6, who are we supposed to trust with all of our heart?

- What do verses 9-10 say will happen if we honor God with our first fruits?

- Read verses 34-35. Who receives mercy and honor?

THINK

- Read verses 3-4. What are the benefits of love and faithfulness?

- Why should we not lean on our own understanding (verse 5)?

- Read verses 11-12. Why would God discipline the people he loves the most?

- Read verses 21-22. How might "sound judgment and discretion...be life for you"?

APPLY

•How does the way you live earn the respect of others? Of God?

•How do you tend to respond to the discipline that comes into your life?

•In what areas of your life do you need to put more trust in God?

DO

Looking at how we spend our money is a really practical way of determining whether we trust God or not. Have the students try this. The next time they receive some money, ask them to set a portion aside to give to your church, to an organization like Compassion International (www.compassion.com), or to someone in need anonymously (make sure they know that means not to let anyone know who it was).

QUIET TIME REFLECTIONS

Day one: Proverbs 3:1-8

1. What word or phrase jumps out to you? Why?

2. How might love and faithfulness win us favor with people?

3. How do you feel about trusting God? Explain.

Day two: Proverbs 3:9-10

1. What word or phrase jumps out to you? Why?

2. Why should we honor God with our wealth?

3. How do you view your material stuff? Is it yours? What kinds of stuff do you desire to buy?

Day three: Proverbs 3:11-12

1. What word or phrase jumps out to you? Why?

2. Who does God discipline?

3. What's the primary purpose of God's discipline? (See also Deuteronomy 8:5 and Hebrews 12:5-6.)

Day four: Proverbs 3:13-18

1. What word or phrase jumps out to you? Why?

2. Why is wisdom so valuable?

3. Define wisdom in your own words.

Day five: Proverbs 3:19-26

1. What word or phrase jumps out to you? Why?

2. What does it mean that "by wisdom the Lord laid the earth's foundations"?

3. What's the benefit of following God's wisdom?

Day six: Proverbs 3:27-35

1. What word or phrase jumps out to you? Why?

2. When are we supposed to do good to others?

3. How do you treat the people around you?

Day seven: Proverbs 3:1-35

Read through the entire passage. Write down the one verse that impacted you the most this week. Commit the passage to memory.

4. DISCOVER BY DOING
Proverbs 4

LEADER'S INSIGHT

I've heard it said everyone finds what he seeks. The author of this proverb seems to offer an axiom: We're either seeking wisdom, which leads to life, or foolishness, which leads to death. Wisdom is seen as supreme. It unlocks the depths of life and leads us where we truly need to go.

We gain wisdom by listening to the people around us who care for us. We struggle in life often because we resist the teachings of God. Our hearts shouldn't be entrusted to just anyone, because they're the wellsprings of life and should be guarded carefully.

"Listen, friends, to some fatherly advice; sit up and take notice so you'll know how to live. I'm giving you good counsel; don't let it go in one ear and out the other" (Proverbs 4:1-2 MSG). When we give our hearts to God, Proverbs 4:12 tells us our "steps will not be hampered." This word *hampered* means a "narrow or cramped situation" (see Isaiah 49:19-20). The idea is, when we seek wisdom, we'll have some space to learn how to live.

If everyone does find what they truly seek, then after reading this proverb, we have to ask ourselves the questions, "What am I seeking? What's most important to me? What do I center my life around? Wisdom and life or wickedness and death?" We discover life by doing – taking action to seek out and discover what's best in life.

SHARE

•What's the most valuable thing you own? What makes it so valuable?

•If you could be an expert at one thing, what would it be? Why?

•Who in your life knows you the best? How did she get to know you so well?

OBSERVE

•According to Proverbs 4:7, what's supreme? What does it cost?

•Read verse 13. Why should we hold on to instruction?

•According to verses 16-19, what's the path of the wicked like? What's the path of the righteous like?

•According to verse 23, why should we guard our hearts?

THINK

•Read verse 6. How can wisdom protect you?

•How is the path of the righteous like the morning sun (verse 18)?

•In verse 19, what does it mean for the path of the wicked to be like deep darkness?

•How is your heart the "wellspring of life" (verse 23 NIV)? How do you guard it?

APPLY

•How good are you at listening to the advice of others?

•Whom do you tend to listen to? Is there a certain type of person you tend to take advice from? Explain.

•If you were to be brutally honest, what path do you see yourself on—the path of the righteous or the path of the wicked?

•How is it challenging to guard our hearts? How well are you guarding your heart? Explain.

DO

Ask students to write letters to themselves. Say something like, Write down all the things you spend most of your time on—the good, the bad, and the ugly. Then write the things you want to be most important to you, things you should center your life around. Give this letter to someone you trust and have him give it to you one year from today to remind you of the things that should be important to you.

QUIET TIME REFLECTIONS

Day one: Proverbs 4:1-9

  1. What word or phrase jumps out to you? Why?

  2. How can wisdom protect you?

  3. What would you be willing to give up to gain wisdom? Explain.

Day two: Proverbs 4:10-13

  1. What word or phrase jumps out to you? Why?

  2. What does it mean to guard instruction? How is it your life?

  3. Do you tend to listen to or rebel against those in authority over you? Explain.

Day three: Proverbs 4:14-17

  1. What word or phrase jumps out to you? Why?

  2. What does the path of the wicked look like?

  3. Do you see yourself on the path of the wise or the destructive?

Day four: Proverbs 4:18-19

  1. What word or phrase jumps out to you? Why?

  2. How would you identify the path of the righteous?

  3. Dawn is a symbol for hope, for a new day. What do you hope in? What do you hope for?

Day five: Proverbs 4:20-23

1. What word or phrase jumps out to you? Why?

2. What are some of the hidden places and issues inside your heart?

3. Why are we so careless with our hearts?

Day six: Proverbs 4:24-27

1. What word or phrase jumps out to you? Why?

2. How do we make level paths for our feet?

3. Are you easily influenced? In good ways or bad ways? What usually influences you and why?

Day seven: Proverbs 4:1-27

Read through the entire passage. Write down the one verse that impacted you the most this week. Commit the passage to memory.

5. PAIN IN THE GUT
Proverbs 5

LEADER'S INSIGHT

Oftentimes children get upset when being corrected or told "no." This is when adults see the screaming, crying, thrashing, and other childish rebuttals to discipline, when a child makes it seem as though her life is over. It's never as bad as it seems, though; that toy or puppy isn't really worth all the screaming, right? The key is perspective.

Proverbs 5 is a reminder of the dangers of choosing to live in our own way. Solomon uses the image of an adulterous woman to illustrate the peril of giving ourselves to something that will lead straight to the grave.

Many believe the adulterous woman is just a representation of idolatry or false teaching, while others take it more literally, as actually speaking of falling into fleshly lust. The power of this temptation is vivid: Her words "drip honey"; her speech is "smoother than oil" (Proverbs 5:3). Either way, this proverb is a stern wake-up call to be careful of the path we choose and the company we walk with. "But in the end she is bitter as gall, sharp as a double-edged sword" (5:4).

The Bible teaches that we'll all be tempted. Some temptations come from Satan (Matthew 4:1-10); others come from our own hearts (James 1:12-15). The letter of James in the New Testament has been compared to the book of Proverbs in its call to practical wisdom on a daily basis. James 1:16 urges us to live carefully and wisely with the admonition: "Don't be deceived."

Solomon, like James, challenged the young man in the proverb to hold fast to his wisdom and "do not turn aside from what I say" (Proverbs 5:7) so he could then enjoy the love of his youth (his first love). Solomon took the perspective of obedience being best and spoke to the reader as a child, pleading with him to welcome discipline and correction.

The reality is, seduction has great power and pull. It takes great wisdom and insight to overcome the temptress. And if we don't? "The lips of a seductive woman are oh so sweet, her soft words are oh so smooth. But it won't be long before she's gravel in your mouth, a pain in the gut, a wound in your heart" (Proverbs 5:3-4 MSG).

SHARE

- When was the first time you remember being disciplined? How did it make you feel?

- What's one rule at school you wish you didn't have to keep? Why?

- When was the last time you gave someone advice or correction to help her? How did she respond?

OBSERVE

- How did Solomon speak to his readers throughout Proverbs 5? What was his tone? What did he consider the reader?

- How is the adulterous woman described in the proverb? Why is she so dangerous?

- Who did Solomon assume sees all the things the reader does in verse 21?

- What are some ways Solomon mentioned to steer clear of this evil (verses 7-9)?

THINK

- In verse 5 what do you think Solomon meant by saying, "her steps lead to the grave"?

- How might the woman's lips and speech be like honey and oil?

- How would you rewrite verses 15-17 in your own words?

- What should you expect to happen if you give in to the adulterous woman?

APPLY

- On a scale of 1 (being poor) and 10 (being good), how well do you receive correction and direction from others?

- In what ways do people give themselves to evil and temptation in our culture? Which things tempt you the most?

- Who helps give you warning and direct you away from temptations in your life?

- Name some paths you shouldn't go near. What types of people might lead you toward destruction and the grave?

DO

Have students try this exercise. Tell them to go to a park or outdoor area near their houses and spend time walking down the paths. Have them ask God to bring to mind the places they need correction and redirection. Remind students to be specific with God and ask for help as they walk. Also tell them to ask someone they respect to help them stay safe and on the right paths for God.

QUIET TIME REFLECTIONS

Day one: Proverbs 5:1-2

1. What word or phrase jumps out to you? Why?

2. Do you think of yourself as wise? Why or why not?

3. By obeying wisdom, do you think you learn to give wisdom? Why or why not?

Day two: Proverbs 5:3-6

1. What word or phrase jumps out to you? Why?

2. What picture comes to mind from verse 3? What picture comes to mind from verse 4? What's the difference?

3. At the end of verse 6, what does the adulterous woman lack?

Day three: Proverbs 5:7-10

1. What word or phrase jumps out to you? Why?

2. What are the implications of verse 8: "do not go near the door of her house"?

3. What are some ways to help you steer clear of temptation's door?

Day four: Proverbs 5:11-17

1. What word or phrase jumps out to you? Why?

2. If you choose not to receive direction and correction, what does verse 11 say will be your reaction in the end?

3. In verse 14 the writer speaks of being ruined in the assembly. Who would notice if you gave in to temptation? Who would be hurt the most?

Day five: Proverbs 5:18-20

1. What word or phrase jumps out to you? Why?

2. Why do you think faithfulness in marriage is so important to God?

3. Do you think God cares about us being fulfilled and satisfied in life? If yes, how so?

Day six: Proverbs 5:21-23

1. What word or phrase jumps out to you? Why?

2. How does verse 21 affect your choices day to day?

3. Take an honest look. Is the way you're living today leading to the consequences mentioned in verses 22-23?

Day seven: Proverbs 5:1-23

Read through the entire passage. Write down the one verse that impacted you the most this week. Commit the passage to memory.

6. WHAT GOD HATES
Proverbs 6

LEADER'S INSIGHT

Every company claims it. Cell phone networks, vehicle manufacturers, computer companies, and landscaping services use this word. Everyone claims to be the most reliable.

Chapter 6 of Proverbs speaks heavily on this idea of reliability. The writer crafted this chapter with a special passion. He used such strong language as troublemaker, scoundrel, and thief to define a person who can't be trusted. Whether such a person promises things he can't deliver or takes something not his, he instantly becomes unreliable. This chapter even has a section where God's top seven least favorite things are listed.

The comparison of humanity's unreliability and God's unfailing character is at the forefront of the chapter. The writer even takes a look at creation to help put life in perspective. Solomon points to ants in verse 6 to give a lesson on hard work and diligence. Proverbs 6:6 states, "Go to the ant, you sluggard; consider its ways and be wise!" This chapter teaches us it's good to plan and be organized—just look at ants.

We don't really have to search too hard to find examples of God's intent for a reliable person. God isn't looking for perfection but faithfulness: "For the eyes of the Lord range throughout the earth to strengthen those whose hearts are fully committed to him" (2 Chronicles 16:9).

We learn in Proverbs the things God hates. He hates violence (3:31), pride (16:5), and injustice (17:15). Proverbs 6:16 teaches six things God hates, seven that are detestable. When we learn what God hates, we also pick up on what he loves.

SHARE

- Have you ever purchased something that was supposed to be reliable but turned out to be worthless?

- Who's the most reliable person in your life? Why?

- How would someone you know well describe you? Do others see you as reliable or unreliable? Why?

OBSERVE

- What's the attitude of the writer to the reader? What words would you choose to describe the relationship?

- What does Solomon say will be the result for troublemakers and villains?

- What does the writer say will help guide the reader and keep her from failing time and time again?

- What's the major danger mentioned in Proverbs 6:20-35? What two reasons are given for this danger being mentioned?

THINK

- In verses 1-3 how has the individual "fallen into [his] neighbor's hands"? What does that phrase mean?

- How does the writer contrast ants and the lazy person in verses 6-11? How are ants an example to us?

- What are the seven things God hates in verses 16-19? Why do you think God hates these things? Which one do you hate the most?

•What other verses in the Bible seem similar to verses 21-23? How might we bind God's Word upon our hearts forever?

APPLY

•What are some ways you've promised something you couldn't follow through on in the past? What kinds of promises are hard for you to keep?

•What grades would you give yourself if the following were qualities on a spiritual report card: Humility, truthfulness, mercy, good deeds, clean intentions, peacemaking?

•How do you think God would grade you—the same or differently? Explain.

•How would you reword verses 27-28 in your own way? Where are you playing with fire in your life?

•What's one area in your life where you could be more reliable to God? What's one step you could take to help you become more reliable?

DO

Have students take calendars and block out one week. During that particular week, ask them to write down one God-pleasing action per day to be accomplished. For example, "I will defend a kid who always gets made fun of" or, "I will avoid gossip."

Have each student share her weeklong schedule with a mentor, parent, or partner and ask that person to keep her accountable to completing the action each day. Students should pay close attention to the emotions they feel as they practice being reliable people for God. Give them this simple warning: Don't allow yourself to become discouraged by a forgetful day. Simply make up for it during the week.

QUIET TIME REFLECTIONS

Day one: Proverbs 6:1-5

1. What word or phrase jumps out to you? Why?

2. In the past week, when was a time you felt trapped by something you said?

3. How can you free yourself from this entrapment? (See also Proverbs 11:15.)

Day two: Proverbs 6:6-11

1. What word or phrase jumps out to you? Why?

2. In what areas of your life do you struggle with laziness?

3. In what ways might not having enough or being poor in some area (for example, money, time, energy, etc.) come from being lazy or lack of planning? Do you feel this in any way in your life now?

Day three: Proverbs 6:12-15

1. What word or phrase jumps out to you? Why?

2. What picture comes to mind when you hear the words *troublemakers* and *villains*?

3. Name a movie where the troublemaker gets what he deserves. Have you ever thought of yourself as a villain? What would you deserve? What has God given you?

Day four: Proverbs 6:16-19

1. What word or phrase jumps out to you? Why?

2. Can God hate something? Is it always wrong to hate something?

3. Is there anything in your life God would hate? Do you agree with God?

Day five: Proverbs 6:20-24

1. What word or phrase jumps out to you? Why?

2. What's your least favorite thing your father or mother always asks you to do? Why does it bother you so much?

3. What's something you've listened to from your parents or someone else you respect that has helped you and saved you from hurt?

Day six: Proverbs 6:25-35

1. What word or phrase jumps out to you? Why?

2. Is anything you're involved in right now dangerous to you?

3. Our rejection of God is often compared to adultery. What's something you could cut out today that would help you surrender more of your life to God?

Day seven: Proverbs 6:1-35

Read through the entire passage. Write down the one verse that impacted you the most this week. Commit the passage to memory.

[From *Studies on the Go: The Book of Proverbs* by Dr. David Olshine. Permission granted to reproduce this page for use in buyer's youth group. Copyright ©2009 by Youth Specialties.]

7. SEX AND THE CITY
Proverbs 7

LEADER'S INSIGHT

Sex. It's everywhere. In almost every magazine ad and TV commercial, we get the vibes. Buying a car, shopping in the mall—we're hit from all angles with the power of seduction. And seduction comes in all shapes and forms: Money, power, popularity, and self-worth. Sex sells.

All 27 verses of chapter 7 describe a young woman dressed to seduce a young man. And who said a book written before the birth of Christ isn't practical?

Looking from his window, the writer of Proverbs unfolds the scene. Scene one reveals the young man "with no sense" making his way through the streets at dark (Proverbs 7:6-9). Scene two (10-20) begins with "then out came a woman to meet him, dressed like a prostitute and with crafty intent, she is unruly and defiant." The final scene is his destruction, starting in verses 21-23, "like an ox going to slaughter, like a deer stepping into a noose, like a bird darting into a snare, little knowing it will cost him his life."

Teens and young adults are extremely vulnerable to sexual temptations. More and more teens are having sex earlier and younger than ever before. God's Word helps us to get a handle and gain perspective on this powerful force. Solomon speaks of a smooth-talking woman, lurking around the corner and spotting a young man "without any sense" (Proverbs 7:7 MSG).

Proverbs 7:13 reads like a romance novel: "She took hold of him and kissed him." Verse 18 says, "Come let's drink deep of love till morning, let's enjoy ourselves with love!" (Check out Rob Bell's *Sex God,* Grand Rapids: Zondervan, 2007. It's a good resource.)

This might be the most important chapter in the Bible for protecting our teens and young adults from sexual landmines before marriage. Let's see what God's Word says about sex and the city.

SHARE

•Have you ever played a trick on someone? Describe it. How did it make you feel? How did the other person respond?

•Name a Christmas present you wanted as a kid.

•What rules did your parents give you as a child that made you feel safe?

OBSERVE

•According to Proverbs 7:1-5, what's the father asking the son?

•Read verses 6-13. Describe the character of the woman and the kind of things she did to seduce the young man.

•How powerful is sexual temptation? How does it make people do foolish things?

•Read verses 21-27. What's the end result of giving into seduction?

•Does seduction really lead to death? How? What other kinds of death might there be other than physical?

THINK

• Do you think most people can handle sexual temptation? Why or why not?

• Why does almost the entire chapter deal with seduction? What's the message here for us? Are there other types of seduction besides sexual? What are they?

• In what ways are we like the young man drawn away by the woman?

• What were some ways the woman led the man astray in verses 10-23?

APPLY

• Where and when do you feel most tempted?

• What are some ways to overcome seduction?

• What types of temptation come after students most frequently?

• What's one practical step you will take in handling temptation?

DO

Bring in some current teenage magazines and have your group look and explore the variety of temptations and seductions that bombard us every day in our world. Then pray as a group, "Lead us not into temptation."

QUIET TIME REFLECTIONS

Day one: Proverbs 7:1-5

1. What word or phrase jumps out to you? Why?

2. What's God trying to tell us about the power of wisdom and overcoming seduction?

3. Spend some time today thinking about some of your most vulnerable areas in life. What are they?

Day two: Proverbs 7:6-13

1. What word or phrase jumps out to you? Why?

2. How is the adulteress described?

3. How does God help us overcome temptation?

Day three: Proverbs 7:14-20

1. What word or phrase jumps out to you? Why?

2. What are some of the ways guys get lured sexually? Girls?

3. In what ways can you guard your eyes and heart?

Day four: Proverbs 7:21-22

1. What word or phrase jumps out to you? Why?

2. How do others' words affect us in the area of being tempted?

3. Think about your words and how they impact others. Write down a couple of examples.

Day five: Proverbs 7:23-24

1. What word or phrase jumps out to you? Why?

2. Why is it important to have wise people in our lives when we face temptations?

3. Who are some of the people you need around you to protect you?

Day six: Proverbs 7:25-27

1. What word or phrase jumps out to you? Why?

2. What's the result of the young man turning his heart toward the young lady?

3. How can we resist becoming victims of sexual seductions or any kind of worldly mistresses?

Day seven: Proverbs 7:1-27

Read through the entire passage. Write down the one verse that impacted you the most this week. Commit the passage to memory.

8. WISDOM AT ITS BEST
Proverbs 8 and 9

LEADER'S INSIGHT

"Street smarts." That's what my parents called it, meaning wisdom that's practical and works in all of life. Who's one of the wisest people you know? "Lady Wisdom" in Proverbs 8 is calling people to embrace wisdom at its best. Proverbs 8:1 says, "Does not wisdom call out? Does not understanding raise her voice?"

In Proverbs 8:10-11 Solomon writes, "Choose my instruction instead of silver, knowledge rather than choice gold, for wisdom is more precious than rubies, and nothing you desire can compare with her." It's a challenge to be wise with money and not get sucked into the trappings of wealth.

Wisdom is more than knowing the right thing. Wisdom is about doing the right thing. And that begins with fearing God and hating evil (Proverbs 8:13). Wisdom is practical and involves hating "pride and arrogance, evil behavior and perverse speech" (8:13).

As we get to know God, we begin to see why wisdom is so important. It leads us to loving what God loves and hating what God hates. God doesn't hate sinners—he hates sin. He doesn't hate people, but he hates how poor choices can ruin lives. Proverbs 9 continues the advice to be wise. Wisdom is used as an analogy of home building in verse 1: "Wisdom has built her house." We've all seen on TV or known someone whose house fell apart because of a poor foundation. We all need the proper foundation for our lives or we'll crack! And how do we get wiser? Proverbs 9:9 states, "Instruct a wise man and he will be wiser still; teach a righteous man and he will add to his learning" (NIV).

Proverbs 8 and 9 will challenge your students to have street smarts—wisdom that works in everyday life.

SHARE

•What is the worst advice you've received?

•What's the best advice you've refused?

•What's the best advice you've followed?

OBSERVE

•What's Proverbs 8:1-21 telling us about wisdom?

•Proverbs 8:22-32 deals with God and wisdom. Do you see any connections with the passage and the coming of the Messiah Jesus?

•What does Proverbs 8:33-36 tell us about a person of wisdom?

•According to Proverbs 9:1-18 who is "Lady Wisdom," and what's she asking of us?

THINK

•Based on Proverbs 8:1-12, why does wisdom's call seem so urgent?

•Proverbs 8:13-21 discusses the fear of God. What does it mean to fear God?

•Proverbs 8:22-32 speaks to the importance of listening to God and other wise people. Why is this crucial? What benefits are listed in these verses?

APPLY

• On a scale of 1 (low) to 10 (high), how wise are you?

• When you need advice, who do you go to and why?

• What types of people do you avoid getting advice from?

• How do you handle criticism? Pout, get angry, listen calmly, some other way?

DO

Have students interview some people "on the street." Tell them to ask some of these questions and report back to your group next week.

a. What does it mean to be wise?

b. Who's the wisest person you know and why?

c. If someone called you wise, what did you do to receive that compliment?

d. What are some ways to obtain wisdom?

QUIET TIME REFLECTIONS

Day one: Proverbs 8:1-11

1. What word or phrase jumps out to you? Why?

2. How is wisdom better than money or fame?

3. Spend some time today thinking about this and write down your answer: If you had to choose between wealth and wisdom, which would you choose and why?

Day two: Proverbs 8:12-21

1. What word or phrase jumps out to you? Why?

2. How does the writer explain the results of counsel and sound judgment?

3. Where in your life do you need sound judgment?

Day three: Proverbs 8:22-32

1. What word or phrase jumps out to you? Why?

2. What are some ways you think God is wise?

3. Spend some time today thinking about some of the foolish decisions and wisest decisions you have made. List some examples.

Day four: Proverbs 8:33-36

1. What word or phrase jumps out to you? Why?

2. What does it mean to "find me" or "fail to find me" here? Is wisdom really a method for finding God?

3. What's most important in your life right now?

Day five: Proverbs 9:1-8

1. What word or phrase jumps out to you? Why?

2. What do you learn about correcting a mocker?

3. Who has saved you from making a foolish choice? How?

Day six: Proverbs 9:9-18

1. What word or phrase jumps out to you? Why?

2. How do you know if you're wise based on this passage?

3. Spend some time today thinking about some decisions you need to make based on listening to God. What are these?

Day seven: Proverbs 8:1-36 and 9:1-18

Read through the entire passage. Write down the one verse that impacted you the most this week. Commit the passage to memory.

9. STICKS AND STONES
Proverbs 10

LEADER'S INSIGHT

Most of us have heard the phrase "sticks and stones may break my bones, but words can never hurt me." When I was a young child, I remember a family friend saying to me, "Sticks and stones may break your bones, and words will ALWAYS hurt you." Based on my experience in life, that version is true. Words can cause us great pain.

In Proverbs 10 King Solomon, the wisest man of all time, shares with us his words of wisdom, words meant not to hurt but to heal us. He uses contrasting statements to show the different outcomes of wisdom and foolishness, diligence and laziness, righteousness and wickedness.

- "Lazy hands make for poverty." (4)

- "Blessings crown the head of the righteous." (6)

- "The wise in heart accept commands." (8)

- "The tongue of the righteous is choice silver." (20)

- "Fools find pleasure in wicked schemes." (23)

- "The lips of the righteous know what finds favor, but the mouth of the wicked only what is perverse." (32)

If we pay attention and apply Solomon's wisdom, we're much less likely to hurt people with sticks and stones or with words.

SHARE

• As a kid, did you ever say to someone, "Sticks and stones can break my bones, but words can never hurt me?" How did he respond?

• How have you used verbal jabs to hurt someone? How did you feel afterward?

• What word or phrase has hurt you the most in the last six months?

OBSERVE

• Read Proverbs 10:8, 10. Now read verses 6 and 11. What do you notice about these verses? Is this significant? Why or why not?

• Notice the blessings of being considered wise and righteous. See if you can discover and name five of those blessings.

• What are the consequences of being found wicked or violent? Can you discover five consequences?

THINK

• In this chapter, what are the two main groups of people? In which group would you place yourself? Why?

• How many times is the concept of blessing referred to in this chapter? To what sort of people is this concept applied?

• Study verse 18. What does it mean to conceal hatred? If you aren't supposed to conceal hatred, what should you do with it? Find Bible verses to support your answer.

• What memories do you have that are blessings? What memories do you wish would disappear from your memory?

APPLY

•Think of someone whom you have hurt with your words. Have you gone to him to restore the relationship? If so, what was his response? If not, what's keeping you from doing that?

•Based on your daily words and actions, are you a righteous person or a wicked person? If you consider yourself a righteous person, what makes you righteous? If you consider yourself a wicked person, are you satisfied being wicked? Why or why not?

•Based on verse 21, what person do you need to encourage? (Solomon uses the word *nourish*.)

•What does it mean to slander someone? Have you ever been slandered? What action steps do you need to take to reconcile with those you may have slandered?

DO

As a group or individuals, make a list of some of the most hurtful and harmful words or phrases you've ever heard. Now make a list of healing and encouraging words or phrases to replace the hurtful and harmful ones. Spend time praying together as a group, asking God to help each of you to use the encouraging and healing words in place of the hurtful and harmful ones.

QUIET TIME REFLECTIONS

Day one: Proverbs 10:1-3

1. What word or phrase jumps out to you? Why?

2. What benefits do you see in these verses for living with integrity? What consequences do you see for being foolish, dishonest, and greedy?

3. Think through your actions and attitudes throughout the day yesterday. Do you bring your parents joy or grief? Spend some time praying through those actions and attitudes. Ask God to help you to love him with all your heart, soul, mind, and strength (Matthew 22:37-38) and to honor your parents (Exodus 20:12).

Day two: Proverbs 10:4-11

1. What word or phrase jumps out to you? Why?

2. What blessings do you see for those who live in integrity, wisdom, and righteousness? What consequences do you see for laziness, meaningless chattering, dishonesty, and violence?

3. How is it hard work to live a life of honesty and integrity?

Day three: Proverbs 10:12-18

1. What word or phrase jumps out to you? Why?

2. What are the different results of hatred and love?

3. How do you typically respond to corrective discipline? What does this passage say heeding discipline will do for you?

Day four: Proverbs 10:19-21

1. What word or phrase jumps out to you? Why?

2. According to this passage, what can you be sure of when you talk constantly?

3. List the differences between the mouth of the righteous and the mouth of the wicked. What are the results of each? Which of the results do you see most in your life?

Day five: Proverbs 10:22-27

1. What word or phrase jumps out to you? Why?

2. List the metaphors used to describe the foolish and the wise in these verses.

3. According to verse 27, what do those who fear God receive from him? What do the wicked receive?

Day six: Proverbs 10:28-32

1. What word or phrase jumps out to you? Why?

2. According to verse 28, what prospect do the righteous have? What happens to the hopes of the wicked?

3. Make a chart with two columns: The righteous and the wicked. Based on verses 28-32, list in each column what is appropriate for each title. What are your thoughts about the differences in each column?

Day seven: Proverbs 10:1-32

Read through the entire passage. Write down the one verse that impacted you the most this week. Commit the passage to memory.

10. CROOKS, CHARACTER, AND CHEERS
Proverbs 11

LEADER'S INSIGHT

What kind of mark do you want to leave behind? What type of legacy do you want to imprint on the world? Nichole Nordeman, a Christian recording artist, sings a song called "Legacy" (*Woven & Spun*, 2002). The chorus goes like this: "I want to leave a legacy. How will they remember me? Did I choose to love? Did I point to You enough To make a mark on things? I want to leave an offering A child of mercy and grace who blessed Your name unapologetically And leave that kind of legacy."

In Proverbs 11 King Solomon provides us with practical wisdom about how to leave a lasting, godly legacy. Throughout the chapter he points out the blessings of following God as well as the damaging effects of living a life of wickedness and greed. Take Proverbs 11:5 for example: "The righteousness of the blameless makes their paths straight, but the wicked are brought down by their own wickedness."

As you study this chapter, ask God to help you understand what kind of legacy you need to pass on to the next generation. Proverbs 11:3, 5-6, and 10 state—

> The integrity of the honest keeps them on track; the deviousness of crooks brings them to ruin. Moral character makes for smooth traveling; an evil life is a hard life. Good character is the best insurance; crooks get trapped in their sinful lust. When it goes well for good people, the whole town cheers; when it goes badly for bad people, the town celebrates. (MSG)

Crooks, character, cheers. Which one do you want to leave behind?

SHARE

•What five words would you want people to say at your funeral to describe you?

•Have you considered your legacy and what you're leaving behind for others to follow? What thoughts and ideas do you have about the kind of legacy you want to leave (and person you want to be)?

•Who in your life has left behind a legacy of godly character? How has her character inspired you to live like she does?

OBSERVE

•According to Proverbs 11:4, what's worthless in the day of wrath?

•According to verses 9, 12, and 13, what power do you have in your tongue?

•What happens to those who give freely (verse 24)? What about those who refresh others (verse 25)? And those who seek what is good (verse 27)?

•What happens to those who bring trouble on their families (verse 29)?

THINK

•According to Proverbs 11, what are the benefits of pursuing righteousness, wisdom, and integrity?

•According to Proverbs 11, what are the consequences of allowing wickedness, laziness, selfishness, and greed to rule your life?

•Why do you think God gives generously to and protects willingly those who are upright and walk in integrity?

•Why do you think God allows the wicked to reap consequences for their actions?

APPLY

•Which of these verses stood out to you with truths you need to see applied to your life?

•Are you known as one who betrays the confidence of others, or do you keep secrets well? Why do you believe this about yourself? Sometime this week ask five people you know well whether you're good at keeping secrets or known for betraying confidences. Ask God to help you with an open heart.

•Which of the areas of wickedness listed in this chapter do you struggle with? What are you doing to overcome this?

•If pride brings disgrace and humility brings wisdom, do you think your life is more filled with disgrace or wisdom?

DO

As a group, compare and contrast the following words: *pride* and *humility*, *diligence* and *laziness*, *generosity* and *greed*, and *righteousness* and *wickedness*. Allow each person in the group to choose one of the positive character traits he wants to focus on allowing God to change in him this week. Have the students choose prayer buddies and commit to pray for and encourage each other throughout the next week. Don't forget to follow up with the group next week about this activity.

QUIET TIME REFLECTIONS

Day one: Proverbs 11:1-3

1. What word or phrase jumps out to you? Why?

2. Give examples of ways that people use "dishonest scales." In what ways have you used "dishonest scales"? Have "dishonest scales" ever been used against you?

3. Have you ever—whether in real life, on TV, in a book, or in the movies—seen pride bring disgrace? Reflect on that situation. What can you do to keep pride out of your life?

Day two: Proverbs 11:4-9

1. What word or phrase jumps out to you? Why?

2. Based on the lifestyle you lead right now, are money and wealth of great importance to you? According to verse 4, what's of value when you stand before God in heaven?

3. What brings down the wicked? What helps the righteous know which way in life is the best way? According to verse 7, what happens to the wicked man when he dies?

Day three: Proverbs 11:10-11

1. What word or phrase jumps out to you? Why?

2. What happens when the righteous are successful? What happens when the wicked die?

3. What do the upright bring to the community around them? What do the wicked bring?

Day four: Proverbs 11:12-17

1. What word or phrase jumps out to you? Why?

2. According to verse 14 what's the best way to make important decisions?

3. Whom does your kindness benefit?

Day five: Proverbs 11:18-23

1. What word or phrase jumps out to you? Why?

2. What kind of person does God delight in? Spend time praying and ask God to help you become that type of person.

3. Think about verse 23. What good comes from pursuing righteousness? What harm comes from wickedness? Contrast the results of giving generously and withholding greedily.

Day six: Proverbs 11:24-31

1. What word or phrase jumps out to you? Why?

2. How many of these verses deal with finances and family provisions?

3. Think about verse 30. Who's considered wise? What daily steps are you taking to attain this type of wisdom?

Day seven: Proverbs 11:1-31

Read through the entire passage. Write down the one verse that impacted you the most this week. Commit the passage to memory.

[From *Studies on the Go: The Book of Proverbs* by Dr. David Olshine. Permission granted to reproduce this page for use in buyer's youth group. Copyright ©2009 by Youth Specialties.]

SECTION TWO

11. LIFELONG LEARNERS
Proverbs 12

LEADER'S INSIGHT

Stephen Covey's bestseller *The 7 Habits of Highly Effective People* (New York: Free Press, 1990) tells us that effective people cultivate a habit of lifelong learning. Proverbs 12 is about being a lifelong learner.

Wisdom is personified in Proverbs as God calling us to himself. We're told in 1 Corinthians 1:30 that Jesus became our wisdom. To experience wisdom and all it offers, we come to God's best gift of wisdom in the person of Jesus Christ.

Wisdom isn't about more school or seminars. It's about knowing God— wisdom is the by-product. In this lesson you'll discover that lifelong learners love discipline. THE MESSAGE says, "If you love learning, you love the discipline that goes with it" (Proverbs 12:1). Lifelong learners listen to advice (12:15) and resist lies. "The Lord detests lying lips, but he delights in people who are trustworthy"(12:22).

Lifelong learners are diligent: "The diligent find freedom in their work; the lazy are oppressed by work. A lazy life is an empty life, but 'early to rise' gets the job done" (Proverbs 12:24, 27 MSG).

Chapter 12 teaches us that being teachable, honest, hardworking, and open to others' rebukes will put us on the road to lifelong learning.

SHARE

•What's the biggest challenge you've experienced in life?

•When have you faced a tough challenge that turned out positive?

•Why do you think some people seem to have more problems than others?

OBSERVE

•Based on Proverbs 12:1-6, what does it take to be a wise person?

•Read verses 7-14. How does one discover how to live right and avoid evil?

•Look at verses 15-21. What seems to be the downfall of a foolish person?

•In verses 22-28, what does God say about diligence and laziness?

THINK

•In verses 1-6, why do we dislike it when people correct and challenge our character?

•What do you think our tongues (what we say) have to do with being wicked or righteous?

•Why do you think Solomon keeps talking about fools (verse 16) in the same breath with the tongue (verses 17-19)?

•In verse 25 why do you think "anxiety weighs down the heart"? How can kind words help relieve worry and stress?

APPLY

•Do you find it easy or difficult to guard your tongue? Why?

•Why is it hard sometimes to tell the whole truth and nothing but the truth?

•Solomon mentions that deceit and anxiety are inside our hearts. What are some ways to discover what's deep down inside of us?

•How do you handle worry and anxiety?

DO

Proverbs 12:1 says, "Whoever loves discipline loves knowledge, but whoever hates correction is stupid." Pass out index cards and have every person write three stupid qualities or decisions teens and adults have or make on the card, like pride, jealousy, gossip, etc. Then have each person read aloud the qualities. After all the readings are completed, encourage each student to take ownership by acknowledging at least one stupid quality in his or her life. After each person admits something stupid in his or her life, read Proverbs 12:1 and affirm that part of being a lifelong learner is acknowledging struggles and failures and listening to correction. Close by praying for a teachable spirit that leads to lifelong learning.

QUIET TIME REFLECTIONS

Day one: Proverbs 12:1-4

  1. What word or phrase jumps out to you? Why?

  2. Why do you think people tend to dislike discipline?

  3. Spend some time today thinking about how you might grow to love discipline.

Day two: Proverbs 12:5-9

  1. What word or phrase jumps out to you? Why?

  2. How does the writer contrast the wicked and the righteous?

  3. Spend some time today thinking about what it takes to be godly without turning people off or sounding "holier-than-thou" (as if you're more holy than they are). Write down your ideas.

Day three: Proverbs 12:10-15

  1. What word or phrase jumps out to you? Why?

  2. Why do the wise listen to advice, whereas fools do what seems right to them?

  3. Whom do you tend to listen to and which people do you choose to ignore?

Day four: Proverbs 12:16-20

  1. What word or phrase jumps out to you? Why?

  2. What wisdom do these verses give us when we're faced with insulting and annoying people?

  3. Spend some time today thinking about this: When do you speak words of healing, and when do you tend to cut others down?

Day five: Proverbs 12:21-24

1. What word or phrase jumps out to you? Why?

2. What do you learn about prudence, and how does that connect with diligence?

3. How might you humbly keep some stuff to yourself rather than be a fool who blurts out information?

Day six: Proverbs 12:25-28

1. What word or phrase jumps out to you? Why?

2. What do you learn about anxiety, righteousness, and immortality? (See also Proverbs 15:13.)

3. Spend some time today thinking about what weighs you down. How you can surrender those issues to Jesus?

Day seven: Proverbs 12:1-28

Read through the entire passage. Write down the one verse that impacted you the most this week. Commit the passage to memory.

12. TONGUE TAMING
Proverbs 13

LEADER'S INSIGHT

"My Stupid Mouth" is sung by John Mayer (*Room for Squares,* 2001). That title would've resonated with King Solomon. Proverbs speaks regularly about the use and misuse of our words. Some researchers say the average teen gets made fun of six times a day. That's 30 jabs per school week and over 1,000 in a year. Put-downs, criticisms, verbal punches, being made fun of, laughed at, and ridiculed. Jesus said in Matthew 12:34, "Out of the overflow of the heart the mouth speaks."

James records—

> The tongue is a small part of the body, but it makes great boasts. Consider what a great forest is set on fire by a small spark. The tongue also is a fire, a world of evil among the parts of the body. It corrupts the whole person, sets the whole course of one's life on fire, and is itself set on fire by hell. (James 3:5-6)

The tongue, though a small part of our body, can cause great havoc and massive destruction.

Proverbs 13 gives a few glimpses into the power of the tongue:

"From the fruit of their lips people enjoy good things." (2)

"Those who guard their lips preserve their lives." (3)

"The teaching of the wise is a fountain of life." (14)

In this session your students will resonate with what Proverbs has to say about the words we speak, how they reflect what's in our hearts, and how we need help taming our tongues.

SHARE

•Why do you think we so easily make fun of people?

•Think of a time you said something hurtful or mean. How did you feel after you said it? Do you wish you could've taken it back?

•What's one of the nicest compliments you've received?

OBSERVE

•Read Proverbs 13:1-6. What do you learn about the tongue and self-control?

•Based on verses 7-12, what can we do when we're in a conflict with someone?

•According to verses 13-19, what can lead us to poverty and shame?

•What's the main idea of verses 20-25 as they relate to who we hang out with?

THINK

•According to verse 2, what do you think it means that "from the fruit of their lips people enjoy good things"?

•Look at verse 3. How does guarding our lips preserve our lives? Aren't some famous people big talkers?

•How does pride create arguments (see verse 10)?

•According to verse 20, how can walking with the wise help us tame our tongues?

APPLY

•When it comes to criticizing others, which one of these best describes you: (A) I take jabs at people regularly; (B) I tend to keep my mouth shut; (C) I tend to gossip more than engage in face-to-face conflict; or (D) I have foot-in-mouth disease and enjoy being critical of others?

•What do you learn about your heart when you speak critically of others?

•What are some ways to guard your heart and mouth?

•Consider what mentor could help you with "mouth" disease. How could you have him help you with this?

DO

Have your group get several Bible concordances and go through as many passages as you can on the tongue or words in the entire Bible. Then spend some time asking God to guard students' lips.

QUIET TIME REFLECTIONS

Day one: Proverbs 13:1-4

1. What word or phrase jumps out to you? Why?

2. Why do you think guarding our tongues is so difficult?

3. How can you spread words of healing instead of hurt? List some ideas.

Day two: Proverbs 13:5-8

1. What word or phrase jumps out to you? Why?

2. How do wealth and poverty relate to righteousness?

3. Spend some time today thinking about your views on money and helping the poor. Write a couple of sentences about your views.

Day three: Proverbs 13:9-12

1. What word or phrase jumps out to you? Why?

2. What does "hope deferred" mean, and how does that make the heart sick?

3. Spend some time today thinking about what your hopes are and how some have happened and others haven't. How do these make you feel?

Day four: Proverbs 13:13-17

1. What word or phrase jumps out to you? Why?

2. What is a trustworthy envoy, and why is communication essential to healing?

3. Spend some time today thinking about people you may have hurt and people who have hurt you. Take some time to pray and forgive them. Seek forgiveness from God for the hurt you've caused and consider whether you need to seek forgiveness from others.

Day five: Proverbs 13:18-22

1. What word or phrase jumps out to you? Why?

2. What might be God's purpose in challenging "good people [to] leave an inheritance for their children's children"?

3. Spend some time today thinking about whether your parents will leave an inheritance for you and your children. Will you leave something for yours? What kind of inheritance will it be?

Day six: Proverbs 13:23-25

1. What word or phrase jumps out to you? Why?

2. According to this passage, what does "spare the rod" mean? Is this a license for discipline? For punishment? Do you think this passage is saying child abuse is okay as discipline? Why or why not?

3. Spend some time today thinking about how parents should discipline their children and teenagers. In your opinion, is spanking children appropriate or not? As a parent, will you spank your children?

Day seven: Proverbs 13:1-25

Read through the entire passage. Write down the one verse that impacted you the most this week. Commit the passage to memory.

[From *Studies on the Go: The Book of Proverbs* by Dr. David Olshine. Permission granted to reproduce this page for use in buyer's youth group. Copyright ©2009 by Youth Specialties.]

13. GETTING ON TRACK
Proverbs 14

LEADER'S INSIGHT

Proverbs is known as wisdom literature, and Proverbs 14 is a good example of why. Throughout this chapter we see many comparisons made between a wise and a foolish person, a wicked or an upright person, a sinful or a righteous person. Some of these verses are making comparisons, while others are stating facts.

Most of the time the verses making the comparisons tell the reader how to live a wise, upright, and righteous life compared to how to live a foolish, wicked, and sinful life. The latter refers to living a life to glorify God and the former a life to glorify self.

What we know about God from the Bible is that he allows humans to choose the lives they want to live. Proverbs 14:12 says, "There is a way that appears to be right, but in the end it leads to death." We have a variety of roads to consider for what appears to be right. Which way will your students go? A life of obedience, or a life of sin? A life centered on God, or on themselves?

Through Christ we have hope, because we can be forgiven and brought back into relationship with God. Those who know Jesus still make foolish choices. We will never be perfect, but through Christ we can work toward maturity and wholeness.

As you dig into Proverbs 14, begin by asking yourself, "Am I leading a life glorifying to God?" This chapter will challenge us to get on track and stay on track with God.

SHARE

•If you could be like anyone you know, who would that be and why?

•Give one example of a wise decision you've made and an example of a bad decision. What were the results of these decisions?

•Why do you think wisdom is so important?

OBSERVE

•Count up how many times the word *but* is used in Proverbs 14. Why do you think this word is used so many times?

•How many verses use the word *wise, upright, righteous, good, foolish, fool, shameful, wicked, evil,* or *sin?* Do you see any patterns with the way these verses are written?

•What do verses 20, 21, and 31 have in common?

•What do verses 2, 16, 26, and 27 have in common?

THINK

•Look again at the verses that mention fools and foolishness. What things make a person foolish? Why is it important to know these things?

•Look at verses 2, 16, 26, and 27 again. How does a person who fears God act? What benefit does a person gain from fearing God?

•Look at verses 17 and 29. What do these verses have in common? What pitfalls could a person avoid by heeding these two verses?

•Read verse 32 and explain what it means by "even in death the righteous have a refuge."

APPLY

•When you read chapter 14, do you feel most of these proverbs are common sense to a person who knows God?

•Why do you think we still struggle with making the same unwise choices?

•Pick one verse or group of verses with the same overall meaning that you feel you personally need to work on. Why?

•What steps can you take this week to begin working toward being the person you know God would like you to be?

DO

Have each person in your group write down a poor choice he or someone else might make on a daily basis. Then have each write down a wise choice a person could've made in that situation. Once everyone has written their comments, have students share with the group. Once everyone has shared, encourage your students to spend some time thinking about some choices they'll be making this week. Then challenge them to think through what the wise choices would be in those situations. Close by praying for each of your students to be aware of where he struggles with unwise choices, and ask God to help him make wise choices.

QUIET TIME REFLECTIONS

Day one: Proverbs 14:9, 11, 32, 34

1. What word or phrase jumps out to you? Why?

2. In these verses, what does it mean to be upright and righteous? Can you think of anyone you know who is upright? Why do you think so?

3. What are some ways you could become more upright and righteous in your daily life?

Day two: Proverbs 14:5, 9, 25

1. What word or phrase jumps out to you? Why?

2. Think about the last time you lied. What motivated you to lie?

3. What are some ways being deceitful could hurt someone else? Whom have you hurt with your deceit? Is there any way you could seek forgiveness for that sin?

Day three: Proverbs 14:20, 21, 31

1. What word or phrase jumps out to you? Why?

2. Read verse 20. What do you think it means when the rich have many friends? Do you know anyone who went from being popular to losing a lot of friends? What happened? Why did she lose her popularity?

3. Can you think of ways you've been mean or unkind to the needy, maybe even those not popular or cool? What are some ways you could respond more to those who are hurting?

Day four: Proverbs 14:17, 29

1. What word or phrase jumps out to you? Why?

2. Verses 17 and 29 speak about a quick-tempered person. What is a quick-tempered person? Do you feel like you are quick-tempered?

3. Think about some ways you could be a more patient person. Identify some people who irritate you and consider how to be more patient with them.

Day five: Proverbs 14:22, 30

1. What word or phrase jumps out to you? Why?

2. What does verse 22 say you receive when you plan what is good or plan what is evil? List some situations when you've done good and received good in return, or when you've done bad and received bad in return.

3. In verse 30, we're told peace gives life, but envy rots the bones. What's the definition of envy? How is envy destructive?

Day six: Proverbs 14:8, 15, 18

1. What word or phrase jumps out to you? Why?

2. After looking at these verses, what would you say is the definition of prudent? What do these verses say a prudent person does?

3. What does a prudent person receive in return for being wise in his choices? In what ways do you think you've acted as a prudent person? In what ways do you need to improve on this?

Day seven: Proverbs 14:1-35

Read through the entire passage. Write down the one verse that impacted you the most this week. Commit the passage to memory.

14. SCHOOL OF HARD KNOCKS
Proverbs 15

LEADER'S INSIGHT

Ever put your hand on a hot stove? I'm guessing it taught you a lesson after screams, burning flesh, and tears! As we study Proverbs 15, you'll see the writer saying sometimes we learn from our mistakes. Experience is a great teacher. No one enjoys this kind of education, but in life we sometimes need to experience failure to grow in wisdom and character. How we respond to this direction is a good sign of whether we're open to it or not. "Stern discipline awaits those who leave the path; those who hate correction will die" (Proverbs 15:10). Proverbs 15 clearly tells us that as followers of God, we have to be pliable and flexible to learn.

Chapter 15, just like chapter 14, continues to have a great deal of contrasts. We see the word *but* 21 times—for example, "A gentle answer turns away wrath, but a harsh word stirs up anger" (15:1). The word *than* appears twice, as in 15:17: "Better a small serving of vegetables with love than a fattened calf with hatred." And *not so* comes up once, in Proverbs 15:7 (NIV). All of these words denote comparisons. This means 24 of the 33 verses in Proverbs 15 are making comparisons. (The other nine are statements of fact.)

Something unique about Proverbs 15 is that it seems to have some clear, overarching themes. As we study this chapter, we'll try to understand why these themes are here and what the writer might be trying to tell the reader. Repetition is always an important part of catching the important themes of the Bible. Be aware of any repetition of words, phrases, or ideas, and in the process, you might learn a thing or two about the school of hard knocks.

SHARE

•Give one example of something you've learned by making a mistake.

•Tell of one time when you said something you regretted saying, maybe because it was said in anger or it hurt someone's feelings.

•Why do you think it's so important to be aware of consequences and outcomes?

OBSERVE

•Look at Proverbs 15:1, 2, 4, 7-8, 23, and 28-29. What do these verses have in common?

•Read verses 5, 10, 12, and 31-32. What's the main theme of these verses?

•What word do verses 7, 11, 13-15, and 28 have in common?

•What theme do you see when you read verses 6, 16-17, and 27?

THINK

•Look back at verses 1, 2, 4, 7-8, 23, and 28-29. What should a wise and righteous person do and not do? Why is this important?

•After looking at verses 5, 10, 12, and 31-32, how should one respond to discipline or correction? Why is it important to respond in the right way?

•Look at verses 10, 19, 21, and 24. The connecting word here is *path* or *course*. Why does a person need to be aware of the path or course he's taking?

•What are verses 7, 11, 13-15, and 28 talking about when they use the word *heart*? Are they talking about a person's physical heart that pumps blood and keeps you alive? If not, what does this word *heart* mean? Why do you think this understanding of heart is important?

APPLY

•Verse 3 tells us the eyes of God are on the wicked and the good. What are some things you wish God hadn't seen you do? Do you have addictions you need to ask God to help you change?

•Do you feel like you're a person who struggles with desiring wealth, material possessions, or popularity? If yes, how does this hinder your walk with God? If no, in what ways has this strengthened your walk with God?

•Look at verses 5 and 20. Have you had anger or hatred toward one or both of your parents recently? Why do you think this is foolish? What would be a good way to respond to your parents' leadership, correction, and discipline?

•Verses 1 and 18 talk about how a person responds in anger. Are you prone to responding harshly and with a hot temper? If so, what are some ways you can work on being more gentle and patient?

DO

After looking at the "school of hard knocks," have your students make a list of ways they're disciplined this week, by their parents, teachers, or someone else in authority over them. Have them write down how they respond to the discipline and what they learn from the experience. They should bring these lists back to the group and briefly share what they learned about themselves and the way they respond to discipline. Then debrief by asking, How are human discipline and God's discipline similar and different?

QUIET TIME REFLECTIONS

Day one: Proverbs 15:1, 2, 4, 7-8, 23, 28-29

1. What word or phrase jumps out to you? Why?

2. When looking at these verses, what should a wise and righteous person do and not do? Why is this important?

3. What are some changes you need to make when it comes to the things you say?

Day two: Proverbs 15:5, 10, 12, 31-32

1. What word or phrase jumps out to you? Why?

2. How do you respond to correction or discipline? Why do you think this is?

3. Think of an older person whom you need to go visit and soak up wisdom from. Who? Why?

Day three: Proverbs 15:7, 11, 13-15, 28

1. What word or phrase jumps out to you? Why?

2. In verse 28 the writer compares the heart of the righteous to the mouth of the wicked. Why do you think the writer would use the heart as the righteous person's guide to what she speaks?

3. If you were to do a heart check right now, what state would you say your heart is in? What are some ways you can improve the state of your heart?

Day four: Proverbs 15:6, 16-17, 27

1. What word or phrase jumps out to you? Why?

2. Look at these verses. What is being pointed out to you in each verse? How are these verses connected?

3. How could you be less concerned about gaining material wealth and more about growing the kingdom of God?

Day five: Proverbs 15:12, 22

1. What word or phrase jumps out to you? Why?

2. Can you think of times you made a bad choice because you didn't listen to or ask for wise counsel?

3. Who are some wise people you could ask for advice when you're making big decisions? What makes them wise?

Day six: Proverbs 15:30-33

1. What word or phrase jumps out to you? Why?

2. Think of the last time someone gave you a cheerful look or good news. Did it bring joy to your heart and health to your soul?

3. What does it mean to heed "life-giving correction"? What about "those who disregard discipline despise themselves"?

Day seven: Proverbs 15:1-33

Read through the entire passage. Write down the one verse that impacted you the most this week. Commit the passage to memory.

15. LEADERSHIP DEVELOPMENT
Proverbs 16

LEADER'S INSIGHT

There are volumes of books, tapes, and resources on leadership. Subjects emerge: "Who is a leader? What is a leader? What does a leader look like? What qualities does it take to become a leader? Are leaders made or born?" Solomon focuses on leadership principles in chapter 16. We learn early in this chapter that God "can't stomach arrogance or pretense" (Proverbs 16:5 MSG). Pride has been the Achilles' heel of many leaders. We've seen many leaders fall sexually, morally, and theologically. Pride goes before destruction according to Proverbs.

Proverbs 16 mentions four qualities about leadership. First, a good leader motivates. He "doesn't mislead, doesn't exploit" (10 MSG). A leader knows where he's going and where he needs to take people. This happens through healthy motivation.

The second quality Solomon mentions is that a good leader abhors "wrongdoing of all kinds; sound leadership has a moral foundation" (Proverbs 16:12 MSG). A godly leader not only hates evil but also desires moral integrity for his followers' lives.

A third characteristic of a good leader is honesty: "Good leaders cultivate honest speech; they love advisors who tell them the truth" (Proverbs 16:13 MSG). My mom taught me when I was young that my word is my bond. Many people don't want to hear the truth, especially about their own lives. Good leaders will surround themselves with truth tellers. Ever been around someone who thinks she's good at something but isn't, and nobody has the courage to speak the truth to her? How many people could we save from a future fall if we would just be honest? Good leaders value the truth.

The fourth gem mentioned in Proverbs 16:15 states, "Good-tempered leaders invigorate lives; they're like spring rain and sunshine" (MSG). A good leader invigorates and refreshes others.

What kind of leader are you? What types of leadership are happening with your group? This chapter helps us sink our teeth into the reality of leadership development.

SHARE

- If you could be president for a week, what changes would you make?

- What do you think is the hardest part of being a leader?

- What do you think is the most important attribute a leader should have?

OBSERVE

- Read Proverbs 16:1-6. What does Solomon have to say about the future?

- According to verses 7-13, what are characteristics good leaders have? What are their actions based on?

- In verses 14-22 Solomon stresses the importance of wisdom. How are leadership and wisdom tied together?

- Based on verses 23-33 what are the causes and effects of our speech? How does our speech affect our relationships with others?

THINK

• Take a look at the first few verses. Do you feel God is guiding your life? If so, how does that affect you on a daily basis?

• Verses 10-17 talk about leadership. How do you think the kings described in these verses are like and unlike God?

• Look at verses 18-20. Why does Solomon warn us about pride?

• Read verses 23-33. Compare and contrast the use of words. What leads us down the wrong path?

APPLY

• Do you feel you're more of a leader or a follower? Explain.

• Do you think being a Christian creates more of a leadership role in life? Why or why not?

• We use words so carelessly today. What are some ways you can choose to speak with wisdom?

• With flared tempers come angry words. What's one step you can take to control your temper and your words?

DO

Have each person think of someone he knows who's in a leadership role. Have each student write down attributes about the person that define the person as a good leader. Then take a few moments to have your students affirm one another and identify some leadership traits and qualities in each person in the group.

QUIET TIME REFLECTIONS

Day one: Proverbs 16:1-5

1. What word or phrase jumps out to you? Why?

2. Think about the plans you make on a daily basis. Do you take any time to ask God about your plans?

3. Think about the word commit. What does it take to help you fully commit to Jesus on a daily basis?

Day two: Proverbs 16:6-11

1. What word or phrase jumps out to you? Why?

2. Do you have anything planned today? Have you run your plans by God yet? Take time to do that.

3. Think about life and your future. How do you feel about the future? Do you seek God's direction for your future, or take it into your own hands?

Day three: Proverbs 16:12-16

1. What word or phrase jumps out to you? Why?

2. Do you rely on your trusted friends for advice? Why?

3. Think about why Jesus was so wise. How would your life be different if you had Jesus' wisdom for a week?

Day four: Proverbs 16:17-21

1. What word or phrase jumps out to you? Why?

2. On a scale of 1 to 5, with 5 being the most, what is your pride level?

3. Think about practical ways to work on living humbly. How would it change you? Do your closest friends see you as humble or proud?

Day five: Proverbs 16:22-28

1. What word or phrase jumps out to you? Why?

2. Have you ever been hurt by gossip? Why is it so easy to fall into that trap?

3. Think about how powerful our words are. Have you ever "killed" someone with your words?

Day six: Proverbs 16:29-33

1. What word or phrase jumps out to you? Why?

2. Do your parents have gray hair? Do you take time to listen and take their advice or blow them off?

3. Think about how God has the final say in our lives. Does that create a desire in you to change? In what areas?

Day seven: Proverbs 16:1-33

Read through the entire passage. Write down the one verse that impacted you the most this week. Commit the passage to memory.

16. WEATHERING RELATIONAL STORMS
Proverbs 17

LEADER'S INSIGHT

Our culture seems obsessed with reality TV. Whether it's following the lives of rich girls in Los Angeles or little people, relational conflict seems to be the centerpiece of the shows.

While we dislike drama in our own lives, we can't seem to stop watching it unfold on the screen. Solomon packs Proverbs 17 with advice on relationships. He begins with the area of conflict: "Better a dry crust with peace and quiet than a house full of feasting, with strife" (1). Proverbs 17 gives advice and warnings to the unwise as to how to conduct their lives and relationships: "The start of a quarrel is like a leak in a dam, so stop it before it bursts" (14 MSG) and "A friend loves at all times, and a brother is born for a time of adversity" (17).

The way we relate to others reveals who God is in our lives. The wisdom given in Proverbs 17 covers a multitude of different kinds of relationships. Isn't it refreshing to have a friend who can at times keep the atmosphere light and even hilarious? That's what Proverbs 17:22 means when it says, "a cheerful heart is good medicine, but a crushed sprit dries up the bones."

Solomon also addresses the parent-child relationship in Proverbs 17:25: "Foolish children bring grief to their father and bitterness to the mother who bore them." Solomon tells us about the wisdom from God and sets the tone for how we should relate to others. It's our turn now to apply that wisdom in our lives and how to weather relational storms.

SHARE

•If you had the chance to be on a reality TV show, would you do it?

•Have you ever shared a room? What were some challenges of sharing space with someone?

•What do you think are some keys to maintaining healthy relationships?

OBSERVE

•Read Proverbs 17:1-6. What does Solomon have to say about the way we speak? Do our words have consequences?

•According to verses 9-14, how do foolish and wise people act differently? How do they respond to different situations? How do your words play into the scenario?

•In verses 15-20 Solomon gives warning about foolishness and our motives. How are these two linked together? What is a motive? What drives a fool? What drives the wise?

•Based on verses 21-28 what's the correlation between how we act and what we say? Is it always best to speak our minds?

THINK

•Take a look at the first few verses. Are you the type to easily argue? Do you feel the need always to be right? If so, how does that affect your relationships with others?

•Read over verses 10-17. What wisdom can you gain from these verses in regards to friendships? What warnings does Solomon give?

•Look at verses 17-21 in THE MESSAGE. How do you think we can marry trouble? Why does Solomon mention relationships between family members?

•Read verses 22-28. Solomon says the wise hold their tongues. Why do you think we often feel the need to say what we think or have the last word?

APPLY

•When conflict arises between you and someone else, how do you most often respond?

•Do you think being a Christian affects how you treat others or respond to conflict? How?

•We use words so carelessly today. What might help you remember to think before you speak?

DO

Take a moment and have each person write down his three most important relationships and how he benefits from them. Have students take a moment to think of ways they could improve their behavior toward or show more love to the people they listed. Then have everyone pray for each of the people on their lists.

QUIET TIME REFLECTIONS

Day one: Proverbs 17:1-5

1. What word or phrase jumps out to you? Why?

2. Making fun of others comes easily, but how does that affect God's heart?

3. Think about what you can do today to put out the fire of gossip. How can you take action to stop gossip?

Day two: Proverbs 17:6-10

1. What word or phrase jumps out to you? Why?

2. Do you have anything planned today? Have you run your plans by God yet?

3. Think about life and your future. How do you feel about the future? How do you seek God's direction for your future?

Day three: Proverbs 17:11-14

1. What word or phrase jumps out to you? Why?

2. Do you rely on your trusted friends for advice? Why?

3. Think about what wisdom means to you. How can you begin to grow in wisdom today?

Day four: Proverbs 17:15-19

1. What word or phrase jumps out to you? Why?

2. Have you ever been through a storm with your family? How did you survive?

3. What do you think it means to be content with what you have? Why do you often desire to get and have more things? Do we really need them?

Day five: Proverbs 17:20-23

1. What word or phrase jumps out to you? Why?

2. On a scale of 1 to 10, with 10 being the most, how selfish are you? How often do you try to make conversations about you?

3. Think about some things that put you in a good mood. How does your mood affect others?

Day six: Proverbs 17:24-28

1. What word or phrase jumps out to you? Why?

2. Think about whom you look up to. Why do you admire these people? Think about whom our culture admires and why. Is there anything wrong with those our culture admires?

3. Do you think you're a positive person? Why or why not? Do others see you as being positive or negative? Why?

Day seven: Proverbs 17:1-28

Read through the entire passage. Write down the one verse that impacted you the most this week. Commit the passage to memory.

[From *Studies on the Go: The Book of Proverbs* by Dr. David Olshine. Permission granted to reproduce this page for use in buyer's youth group. Copyright ©2009 by Youth Specialties.]

17. HANDLING CRASHES
Proverbs 18

LEADER'S INSIGHT

Ever been in a crash? I'm not speaking of a car crash, but a relational one. These personality clashes can be painful. It's no wonder we sometimes avoid people. Conflict is inevitable. Maybe the Beatles understood this when they wrote the song "Eleanor Rigby": "All the lonely people, where do they all come from, all the lonely people, where do they all belong?" (*Revolver*, 1966) They belong alone because maybe they're tired of the headaches of relationships.

Inside each of us is a battle of two tales: To desire and to hide. We have the tension going on all the time, wanting relationships but also wanting to hide. We want to know and be known but we also want to hide and run away. Inside us is the fear of being loved, vulnerable, and transparent.

The first human couple, Adam and Eve, after they chose to disobey God's plan, heard God call, "Where are you?" Adam responded, "I heard you in the garden, and I was afraid...so I hid" (Genesis 3:9-10). Adam feared and then hid. And so do we.

Proverbs 18:1 begins with a crash of sorts: "An unfriendly person pursues selfish ends and against all sound judgment starts quarrels." Later on in verse 6 we are told the "lips of fools bring them strife, and their mouths invite a beating." Proverbs 18:7-8 states, "The mouths of fools are their undoing, and their lips are a snare to their very lives. The words of gossip are like choice morsels; they go down to the inmost parts."

Proverbs 18:13 says, "To answer before listening—that is folly and shame," and finally in verses 20-21 we read, "From the fruit of their mouths people's stomachs are filled; with the harvest of their lips they are satisfied. The tongue has the power of life and death, and those who love it will eat its fruit." This chapter is filled with proverbs about conflicts.

All relationships involve conflict. It's inevitable, but that doesn't always have to be a bad thing. Fearful of the crash? In this session we'll get a grip on handling crashes.

SHARE

- If you could watch one chick flick over and over, which one would it be and why?

- What are some of the reasons people crash in their relationships?

- In our imperfect world what would a healthy relationship be like? Would the couple have conflicts and crashes?

OBSERVE

- Read Proverbs 18:1-6. What do you learn about foolishness and wisdom?

- Based on verses 7-14, what does God teach us about humility and pride?

- Look at verses 15-19. How should we resolve conflict?

- What are verses 20-24 saying about the words we speak and the impact those have on relationships?

THINK

• Why do you think verses 1-6 deal with relational problems?

• Based on verses 7-14, what do you think are some certain steps to become more humble?

• Look at verses 15-19. Why do you think solving a problem with someone else is really hard?

• Read verses 20-24 and think about the way you choose your words wisely or foolishly. Would you be willing to share an example of either with the group?

APPLY

• What are some practical ways to turn away from gossip, according to verse 13?

• Verses 13, 15, and 17 give some advice on dealing with relational crashes. What are they, and how are you doing with this perspective?

• Do you think verse 22 is saying marriage is a good thing and singleness is bad—or a lesser choice? What do you think?

• How many friends, based on verse 24, should we have, and how can we handle too many or too few?

DO

Have students take this inventory. Say something like, Think about how you normally respond when you get stuck in a conflict, not how you wish you would respond. Choose the top two that describe you. These statements are meant to create an open discussion.

When I am faced with conflict...

A. I like to get my own way in the argument.

B. I become the martyr and let the other person win.

C. I throw a pity party.

D. I pretend there is no problem to avoid conflict.

E. I interrupt a lot.

F. I bring up past issues.

G. I take things personally and have a hard time forgiving.

Discuss:

•What do you think might be motivating you to react this way?

•How might you respond in a more positive way during a conflict?

QUIET TIME REFLECTIONS

Day one: Proverbs 18:1-4

1. What word or phrase jumps out to you? Why?

2. Why do you think some people are so overconfident and opinionated?

3. How open are you to others' opinions?

Day two: Proverbs 18:5-8

1. What word or phrase jumps out to you? Why?

2. When it comes to issues of justice, what are you most passionate about? What injustices make you most angry?

3. Spend some time today thinking about ways you can make a difference in a world of injustice. List some ideas.

Day three: Proverbs 18:9-12

1. What word or phrase jumps out to you? Why?

2. What tends to cause people to become proud?

3. Spend some time today thinking of ways or situations in which you get arrogant. How can you grow in humility?

Day four: Proverbs 18:13-16

1. What word or phrase jumps out to you? Why?

2. What are the destructive results of not fully listening to people?

3. Spend some time today thinking about your listening skills. Do you stay engaged? Interrupt? Tune out?

Day five: Proverbs 18:17-20

1. What word or phrase jumps out to you? Why?

2. What are some of the ways we offend our friends?

3. Spend some time today thinking about someone you've hurt in the past. If you could talk with her now, what would you say?

Day six: Proverbs 18:21-24

1. What word or phrase jumps out to you? Why?

2. Think about the ways our tongues give life or death. What's an example?

3. How do the following conditions affect your words:

   (a) extreme tiredness?

   (b) agitation?

   (c) anger?

   (d) depression?

   (e) _____

Day seven: Proverbs 18:1-24

Read through the entire passage. Write down the one verse that impacted you the most this week. Commit the passage to memory.

18. ACCEPTING CORRECTION
Proverbs 19

LEADER'S INSIGHT

Ever wondered why people get mad at God for things that are their own fault? Proverbs 19:3 says, "People ruin their lives by their own stupidity, so why does God always get blamed?" (MSG) Our own stupidity, according to Solomon, is what gets us into trouble. So why does God get all the blame when it's our fault? Your students shouldn't be surprised that when they make poor choices and bad decisions, it opens the door for others to be critical of them—which leads often to some kind of confrontation.

Proverbs uses words like *correction* and *rebuke* and the phrase "listen to advice." It's really hard to hear someone tell it like it is. "You can't handle the truth" is the famous line uttered by Jack Nicholson's character in the movie *A Few Good Men* (1992). But Proverbs says when we're open to hearing the truth, we'll grow: "Listen to advice and accept discipline, and at the end you will be counted among the wise" (19:20).

God is telling us if we can handle the truth about ourselves, we're going to experience the blessings of joy and insight. We also learn about the pitfalls of rejecting God's correction in Proverbs 19: "Stop listening to instruction, my child, and you will stray from the words of knowledge" (27). In this session let's help our students learn about accepting correction.

SHARE

- If a friend were doing something you disliked, would you say anything, or remain quiet?

- Can you name a time when someone said something truthful to you that was hard to hear?

- What's one correction you hear frequently from your parents?

OBSERVE

- Read Proverbs 19:1-7. What's God saying about wealth and poverty and how those affect relationships?

- What do verses 8-13 teach us practically about wisdom in this passage?

- Look at verses 14-21. What do you learn about listening to others' advice?

- Verses 22-29 deal with relationships. From verse 27, how do we stray from words of knowledge?

THINK

- Verse 4 stresses that people are drawn to money, and the poor get deserted. Why do you think this happens?

- What do you think verse 8 means when it says, "Those who get wisdom love their own lives." What does it mean to love your own life?

- Compare and contrast verses 13, 18, and 20. What do these have to do with receiving correction?

- Explain verses 25-27 and how they relate to spiritual growth.

APPLY

•Have you ever found yourself getting close to the rich and deserting the poor? How?

•What's God's perspective of the poor based on verse 17, and how can you have the same heart?

•What's the blessing mentioned in verse 20, and why do we tend not to listen?

•What's the difference, according to verse 25, between learning from criticism and refusing correction? How can you benefit from this passage?

DO

Play the affirmation game. Put one of the students in the group in the middle. Have group members tell the student in the middle these two things:
1. The thing I appreciate about you is...
2. You make our group better by...

QUIET TIME REFLECTIONS

Day one: Proverbs 19:1-5

1. What word or phrase jumps out to you? Why?

2. What do you think "desire without knowledge is not good" means? (verse 2)

3. Spend some time today thinking about some ways you "miss the way" because of "hasty feet" (verse 2). Write down some of them.

Day two: Proverbs 19:6-11

1. What word or phrase jumps out to you? Why?

2. Why does the writer insist that a person's wisdom yields patience?

3. How can you grow in the area of patience with God, yourself, and others?

Day three: Proverbs 19:12-15

1. What word or phrase jumps out to you? Why?

2. How might a child ruin the relationship with his father?

3. What are some ways you're foolish in your relationships with your parents?

Day four: Proverbs 19:16-20

1. What word or phrase jumps out to you? Why?

2. What kind of penalty does the hot-tempered person receive? How can we help someone who's angry?

3. Spend some time today thinking about what gets you angry. Do you get angry about things that don't matter?

Day five: Proverbs 19:21-24

1. What word or phrase jumps out to you? Why?

2. What does it mean that the person who fears God is untouched by trouble?

3. How can you learn to fear God?

Day six: Proverbs 19:25-29

1. What word or phrase jumps out to you? Why?

2. How do verses 25-27 relate to being open to correction?

3. Spend some time this week working on being a good listener when your parents and friends correct you. Describe any times you tried this.

Day seven: Proverbs 19:1-29

Read through the entire passage. Write down the one verse that impacted you the most this week. Commit the passage to memory.

19. HONEST TO GOD?
Proverbs 20

LEADER'S INSIGHT

"To tell the truth and nothing but the truth" is the pledge people make as they testify in a court of law. Proverbs 20 speaks to us about honesty, whether in our relationships with God, our family, neighbors, friends, or people at work or school. Students know how tough it is in our culture to be forthright and honest.

What keeps us from being honest with ourselves? What roadblocks do we put between ourselves and our friends in the honesty category? Why are we afraid to be real with God?

In this session we learn from Proverbs 20:7 that children who follow the integrity of their parents will be blessed. Verse 10 teaches that "differing weights and differing measures—the Lord detests them both." THE MESSAGE states it this way: "Switching price tags and padding the expense account are two things God hates." Proverbs 20:17 instructs that "food gained by fraud tastes sweet, but one ends up with a mouth full of gravel."

God is saying he detests dishonesty! Even in the area of money, God says, "An inheritance claimed too soon will not be blessed in the end" (Proverbs 20:21). God despises dishonesty and honors and delights in truthfulness. "The Lord detests differing weights, and dishonest scales do not please him," says Proverbs 20:23. "God hates cheating in the marketplace" (23 MSG).

The bottom line is, God wants us to develop integrity, so what we're really like when no one is looking lines up with how we are in public.

That means being brutally honest with our lives, our sin, our material stuff, our personal addictions, and our habits and getting honest with God. When we get real with people, real with ourselves, and real with God, people will feel safe with us. Honest to God!

SHARE

•What is the biggest lie you've ever told?

•How does it make you feel when someone is dishonest with you?

•What's the best way to handle someone who lies to you?

OBSERVE

•What does Proverbs 20:1-8 have to do with integrity and honesty?

•Read verses 9-16. How does the passage relate to being honest with God?

•Look at verses 17-23. What's the theme here about differing weights? (See also verse 10.)

•What do verses 24-30 say about allowing God to search our hearts?

THINK

•What is verse 1 saying about the use of alcohol? What does it mean to be led astray?

•Why do you think the lazy (sluggards) seem to struggle in life and the diligent make it?

•A differing weight refers to the loaded scales a merchant would use to cheat his customers. How are people cheated in today's world?

•What do integrity and dedication, mentioned in verse 25, have to do with honesty?

APPLY

•What are some ways to avoid being a sluggard?

•Who do you relate more to: The one being cheated or the one cheating someone else?

•How do you feel when you've been lied to? How do you feel after lying to someone? Which in your mind is worse?

•What are some ways to honor your parents so your "lamp" will not be "snuffed out"?

DO

Do a spontaneous drama. Have students create some quick dramas developing some of the scenarios listed. They can be short (one to three minutes).

A. Becky lies to her parents about leaving school property early.

B. Jennifer tells her best friend she isn't dating Will when she really is.

C. Ben is irritated with his best friend C. J. but doesn't want to tell him what's bothering him.

D. Joel is afraid of letting his youth pastor know he might not believe in God.

QUIET TIME REFLECTIONS

Day one: Proverbs 20:1-5

  1. What word or phrase jumps out to you? Why?

  2. How do you avoid strife?

  3. How might you seek the wisdom God is placing in your heart (see verse 5)?

Day two: Proverbs 20:6-10

  1. What word or phrase jumps out to you? Why?

  2. When was the last time you felt sinful or sinless?

  3. Spend some time today praying and confessing your sins to God.

Day three: Proverbs 20:11-15

  1. What word or phrase jumps out to you? Why?

  2. How do your actions affect other people?

  3. What motivates you to be dishonest with people?

Day four: Proverbs 20:16-20

  1. What word or phrase jumps out to you? Why?

  2. Why do we often avoid seeking guidance and advice from others?

  3. Who is the one person you trust the most?

Day five: Proverbs 20:21-25

1. What word or phrase jumps out to you? Why?

2. How does living our own way apart from God cause us to lose direction?

3. In what areas of life do you need direction from God?

Day six: Proverbs 20:26-30

1. What word or phrase jumps out to you? Why?

2. Proverbs 20:29 affirms the strength of youthfulness and the gray hair as a symbol of wisdom for the aging. Which older person do you respect the most?

3. Spend some time today thinking about someone in her 50s or 60s whom you could learn a great deal from. What are some steps you can take to learn from this person?

Day seven: Proverbs 20:1-30

Read through the entire passage. Write down the one verse that impacted you the most this week. Commit the passage to memory.

20. WHY YOU DO WHAT YOU DO
Proverbs 21

LEADER'S INSIGHT

Many students and adults do good deeds. And yet, why do these things? Is it to be seen by others? To show off how spiritual we are? Proverbs 21 focuses on the issue of motives: Why we do what we do.

Jesus frequently spoke against hypocrisy. In Matthew 23 seven times Jesus said "woe" to the religious leaders, known as the Pharisees. He rebuked them for publicly showing off and doing deeds to receive praise from people rather than from God. Jesus said, "But do not do what they do, for they do not practice what they preach. Everything they do is done for people to see." (Matthew 23:3, 5)

Proverbs 21:2 states, "People may think all their ways are right, but the Lord weighs the heart." God knows not only what we do, but also why we do it. Humans base things on the exterior; God examines the interior (1 Samuel 16:7).

Why are motives so important? It's easy for us to notice what's wrong with the world, but difficult actually to do something about it. Why? Does this relate back to our motives? The author in Proverbs 21 is challenging us to be people of action, doing what's right and just rather than just talking about it: "When justice is done, it brings joy to the righteous but terror to evildoers" (15). God tells us to pursue "righteousness and love," resulting in finding "life, prosperity and honor" (21).

The question we must ask ourselves is, are we making the world a better place, or are we just adding to the noise? Before you act, ask God to examine your motives.

This chapter teaches us to make sure our good works aren't coming from a need to be liked or to display how religious we are. We shouldn't let fear keep us from doing the right thing but ask God to guard our hearts—that way we'll be able to discern why we do what we do.

SHARE

•Have you ever heard someone say, "Do as I say, but not as I do"? How does that make you feel?

•What are some ways you can tell if someone really values something?

•Have you ever done something nice for someone anonymously? How did it make you feel?

OBSERVE

•According to Proverbs 21:2, what does God weigh?

•Read verse 3. What's more acceptable to God?

•From verse 21, if someone pursues righteousness and love, what does he find?

•According to verse 31, where does victory rest?

THINK

•Why is doing what's right and just more acceptable than sacrifice?

•How might a gift given in secret soothe someone's anger?

•In verse 20 what's the difference between the wise and the fool?

•Read verse 23. How does guarding your mouth keep you from calamity?

APPLY

•Are you the kind of person who does what you say? Explain.

•Does the way you speak reflect your heart? Explain.

•Do you know someone who could specifically use your help? How could you help her?

•Is it hard to practice what you preach? Why?

DO

Have students try this exercise this week. Explain by saying something like, You receive an incredible sense of satisfaction when you anonymously do something for someone. Plan a "random acts of kindness" week for you and a friend. Schedule a random act of kindness for each day of the week. Keep the acts anonymous; only you and your friend can know about the kind things you do. After each act, debrief with your friend, discussing what impact your kind act made on those you did it for.

QUIET TIME REFLECTIONS

Day one: Proverbs 21:1-3, 12, 21, 27, 30-31

1. What word or phrase jumps out to you? Why?

2. Why would doing what's right and just be more acceptable to God than sacrifice?

3. Why do you think God desires for us to be people who pursue righteousness and love?

Day two: Proverbs 21:4-8, 20

1. What word or phrase jumps out to you? Why?

2. What does *diligent* mean? How might diligence lead to profit?

3. Are you a hasty person? Explain.

Day three: Proverbs 21:9, 19

1. What word or phrase jumps out to you? Why?

2. Why would it be better to live on the corner of a roof or in a desert than with a quarrelsome wife?

3. Do you consider yourself someone who is quarrelsome? Explain.

Day four: Proverbs 21:13-15

1. What word or phrase jumps out to you? Why?

2. How might a gift given in secret soothe anger?

3. How might justice bring joy to the righteous and terror to evildoers?

Day five: Proverbs 21:16-18, 28-29

1. What word or phrase jumps out to you? Why?

2. How might straying from the path of understanding lead you into the company of the dead?

3. What does it mean to put up a bold front?

Day six: Proverbs 21:22-26

1. What word or phrase jumps out to you? Why?

2. How does guarding your tongue keep you from calamity?

3. Do you see yourself as a generous person? Why or why not?

Day seven: Proverbs 21:1-26

Read through the entire passage. Write down the one verse that impacted you the most this week. Commit the passage to memory.

SECTION THREE

21. GUIDELINES FROM ABOVE
Proverbs 22

LEADER'S INSIGHT

I love cheesecake. And chocolate chip cookies hot out of the oven. I'm pretty sure most people love some type of sweets. The ingredients you put into a pie will have a lot to do with how good the pie tastes after you bake it.

Our lives kind of work the same way. What we do and how we live are similar to the ingredients of a pie; they can determine how good our lives can taste. The author in Proverbs 22 wants us to understand that the choices we make and the things we do have an impact on the lives that we live.

Proverbs 22 gives us a few ingredients for godly living. The first ingredient is to handle our money and possessions wisely. Solomon was the wealthiest person in his day as the king of a massive empire. In fact, after he built a temple for God, Solomon also built a palace for himself. Here's what the New Living Translation says in 1 Kings 7:1: "Solomon also built a palace for himself, and it took him thirteen years to complete the construction." It's hard to fathom that Solomon, after building a temple, also built himself another big "crib" (home).

The Bible tells us the love of money is a root of all kinds of evil (1 Timothy 6:10). God tells us riches can get in the way of our faith (1 Timothy 6:6-16). Godliness with contentment is great gain. The Bible says the generous will be blessed (Proverbs 22:9). Life is about generosity. It's about giving, not receiving. Be generous. I think Solomon learned this lesson eventually.

The second ingredient is to trust in God wholeheartedly (Proverbs 22:20). The name of God is a strong tower. When life gets hard, God desires us to lean on him.

Proverbs 22 provides a third ingredient for godly living: Don't make friends with angry and abusive people (verses 24-25). God's goal is for us to live abundant lives. He wants us to live the way he intended life to be: God's way, with his ingredients. Let's look into the guidelines from above and what we learn about God in the process.

SHARE

- What's something you're good at? How would you get better at it?

- Do you believe in the saying "Practice makes perfect"? Why?

- If you could change your name to anything, what would you change it to? Why?

OBSERVE

- According to Proverbs 22:9, why will the generous man be blessed?

- Read verses 17-18. Why pay attention to the wise sayings, and why should we apply them to our hearts?

- According to verses 24-25, why shouldn't we make friends with a hot-tempered man?

THINK

- What goes into a good name? Why is it more desirable than great riches?

- How might humility and fear of God bring wealth and honor and life?

•What does verse 18 mean when it says, "It is pleasing when you keep them in your heart"?

•What does it mean for folly to be bound up in the heart of a child? How might discipline drive folly from a child?

APPLY

•Do you believe you have a good name? Explain.

•How do you answer when people ask why you live the way you do?

•When people say your name, what do you think comes to mind? What would you like to come to mind?

DO

Pass out pieces of paper with these verses on them or list the verses on a whiteboard or overhead, then have students break up into smaller clusters to identify what they notice about God's nature in the verses.

Proverbs 11:8, 21; 13:13; 15:3, 11; 16:33; 17:5; 19:16; 21:27, 30; 28:9

QUIET TIME REFLECTIONS

Day one: Proverbs 22:1, 4, 8, 12

   1. What word or phrase jumps out to you? Why?

   2. Why would a great name be more desirable than riches?

   3. What do you think people think about when they hear your name?

Day two: Proverbs 22:2, 9, 16, 22-23

   1. What word or phrase jumps out to you? Why?

   2. How will a generous man be blessed by sharing?

   3. How do you view people who are less fortunate? Do you see them as equals? Explain.

Day three: Proverbs 22:3, 5, 7, 14, 17-21

   1. What word or phrase jumps out to you? Why?

   2. What's the benefit in paying attention to the sayings of the wise?

   3. Are you quick to listen to the advice of people who are wiser than you?

Day four: Proverbs 22:6, 15, 28

   1. What word or phrase jumps out to you? Why?

   2. How does discipline drive out folly?

   3. How do you tend to react to discipline?

Day five: Proverbs 22:10-11, 24-25

1. What word or phrase jumps out to you? Why?

2. What is a mocker? Why would a mocker's absence remove strife, quarrels, and insults?

3. What's the danger of being a hot-tempered person?

Day six: Proverbs 22:13, 26-27, 29

1. What word or phrase jumps out to you? Why?

2. What's the danger in getting in debt to other people?

3. Do you find yourself making promises you can't keep to people? Explain why or why not.

Day seven: Proverbs 22:1-29

Read through the entire passage. Write down the one verse that impacted you the most this week. Commit the passage to memory.

22. THE DANCING HEART
Proverbs 23

LEADER'S INSIGHT

My wife, son, and I dance every night before bedtime. It's hilarious, and I hope nobody videotapes it. It's really fun, especially since I'm bad at it! *Dancing with the Stars* would never give me an audition.

What makes you dance in life?

Why are rewards given to people who return a lost dog to its owner? Why does a car insurance company offer benefits for safe drivers? Why are students given scholarships for good grades? In each of these three scenarios, the success should actually be the reward itself. For someone to return a lost dog, the reward is being an honest person—and for a student with good grades the reward is a good education. Rewards are positive, but the question should be raised: Shouldn't people be motivated by the reward of doing right without external rewards?

Proverbs 23 dissects this question perfectly by posing 13 different sayings related to self-restraint. Each saying deals with questions of money, power, fame, disobedience, alcohol, words, and even property lines. Whatever the topic, the conclusion is the same. To be self-restrained is honoring to God.

Proverbs 23:15-16 says the outcome of living in control is a glad and joyous heart. The heart of a self-restrained person is bright, guilt-free, and alive. The writer of Proverbs is clearly communicating the benefits of living a clean and pure life.

So next time a reward is offered for doing the right thing, don't take it! Serve with a dancing heart, knowing you're making a choice to become a person of godly action and restraint. Go ahead—do a two-step!

SHARE

- Shopping, ice cream, gossip, cell phone, computer—what's the hardest item on this list for you to resist? Why?

- Why is it so difficult to restrain from some things and not others?

- When was the last time you had to show self-restraint? Explain.

OBSERVE

- How many times does the phrase "do not" show up in Proverbs 23?

- What are the two body parts used to describe the need for obedience in verse 12? What are these body parts supposed to be doing?

- From verses 15 and 16, what will make the writer's heart so glad and excited?

- What in verses 29-35 is said to be so dangerous? What is the possible outcome of this danger?

THINK

- Why are a person's heart and ears important, according to verse 12? How do you accomplish these two instructions?

- How would you rewrite verse 23 in your own words?

- What's the reward offered in verses 15-16? Does this reward motivate you?

APPLY

• When was the last time you felt like you received a reward for making a right choice before God? Was it worth it?

• What word of advice from chapter 23 do you relate to most? Why?

• Would those who are closest to you say the way you live causes their hearts to dance? Why or why not?

• What are times in your life where you were rewarded by restraining from something? What was the reward?

DO

Read Jesus' words in Matthew 6:2-4, 6:5-6, and 6:16-17. Have students pay attention to the use of the phrase "they have received their reward in full." The individuals who took part in these three incredibly selfless things made the actions into selfish ventures. Their reward was their own egos being inflated. During the next week have students practice these three activities without drawing attention to what they're doing: Helping those in need, praying in secret, and fasting from food. Ask students to write down the rewards they receive from each activity.

QUIET TIME REFLECTIONS

Day one: Proverbs 23:1-5

1. What word or phrase jumps out to you? Why?

2. What activities did you do today seeking to be fulfilled (for example, eating, sleeping, etc.)? Did they bring you satisfaction? How did they leave you wanting more?

3. What ways does God provide fulfillment for you?

Day two: Proverbs 23:6-9

1. What word or phrase jumps out to you? Why?

2. How might you reprioritize your life to better spend your time?

3. Have you ever been a begrudging host? What happened? Did you learn anything?

Day three: Proverbs 23:10-14

1. What word or phrase jumps out to you? Why?

2. How do you normally respond to discipline? Is there any advice you didn't receive well that you should've listened to?

3. Have you had any times in your life when instruction or discipline you received saved your life? When? Describe what happened.

Day four: Proverbs 23:15-21

1. What word or phrase jumps out to you? Why?

2. When is a time you know you made your parents happy with a decision you made? How did that make you feel?

3. In the past week have you envied someone who doesn't live for God? What did you envy?

Day five: Proverbs 23:22-28

1. What word or phrase jumps out to you? Why?

2. In verse 23 the writer instructs the reader to buy truth. What does this mean? How much of your bank account is being spent on truth, and how much is being spent on things that promote lies?

3. Where are you giving your attention and affection today?

Day six: Proverbs 23:29-35

1. What word or phrase jumps out to you? Why?

2. Does verse 29 describe how you feel in any way? Why or why not?

3. Are there any cravings in your life like those described in verses 30-35? Does anything control you that Jesus would want to free you from?

Day seven: Proverbs 23:1-35

Read through the entire passage. Write down the one verse that impacted you the most this week. Commit the passage to memory.

23. FALLING TO PIECES
Proverbs 24

LEADER'S INSIGHT

Chances are some adult has used the timeless cliché "If your friends jumped off a bridge, would you do it, too?" with at least one of your students. Every youngster is tempted to respond in a notorious way by stating he would, but he'd bring a parachute. But the question begs real consideration. How easily are we swayed by others? How quickly do we give in to negative peer pressure? Are we capable of making wise choices on our own? In life we really have only two ways of living, either wisely or foolishly. Either path leads to consequences, and we should take these into account as we decide which path to walk in life.

Proverbs 24 addresses the benefits of choosing to live in God's ways: "By wisdom a house is built, and through understanding it is established; through knowledge its rooms are filled with rare and beautiful treasures" (2). The writer points out the coming destruction and disapproval of God for those who scheme to do evil and influence others to do evil. According to Proverbs 24, deciding to do the right thing demonstrates wisdom.

Proverbs 24:10 states, "If you falter in a time of trouble, how small is your strength." THE MESSAGE says it more emphatically: "If you fall to pieces in a crisis, there wasn't much to you in the first place." The advice in Proverbs 24 is this: Build your life on God's wisdom, and the by-product will be a renewed strength in God and an ever-increasing understanding of who you are and who God is. The warning in Proverbs 24 is: Don't jump off a cliff—don't fall to pieces. Choose the fear of God instead (verse 21).

SHARE

• Who's the wisest person you know? Why do you consider her to be wise?

• When was the last time you were influenced to do something you regretted later?

• What would be the most difficult thing for you to give up for two weeks? Why?

OBSERVE

• Why does Proverbs 24:1 warn against envying the wicked or desiring their company?

• What's God saying to us in verses 5-12 about the choices we make?

• What's wisdom compared to in verses 13 and 14? What does this sweet discovery lead to?

• What do verses 30 and 31 say is the outcome for a person who's lazy and has no wisdom?

THINK

• What's the "assembly at the gate" in verse 7? Why does it say fools "must not open their mouths" at the assembly? What gives someone the right to speak?

• Why is there a command in verses 17-18 not to gloat in the failure of your enemies? What does this show about you if you do gloat?

• What does verse 26 bring to mind? How would you reword that verse based on your own understanding?

• In verses 31-34 why does the property of the fool fall into disrepair? What's the implication of this in your life?

APPLY

•Think of your plans last week. Did any of them resemble evil plots? Were any of them selfish plots? Hateful plots? Foolish plots?

•What's a piece of wisdom you've been offered but refused to see as tasty honey? What future hope might come by obeying this wisdom?

•How do you feel after you make a foolish decision? How do you feel after you make a wise decision?

•When was the last time you tried to rescue a friend "staggering toward slaughter" or personal destruction?

DO

Have each student make a "wisdom pack" for the week ahead. Explain it with something like, Simply look up seven Scriptures that strike you as passages full of future hope and helpful wisdom. Write each verse down on a small note card or sticky note for each day. Each morning pull from your wisdom pack one of the cards (make it random...just pull the first one you come to) and commit that verse to memory for the day. Place the card somewhere you'll see it constantly. Think about this: Does that day's card minister to you in some kind of way? Does it seem appropriate for your day? Does it bring about hope for your day? After the week is over, display the cards by making a framed piece of art full of color and pictures to make a beautiful reminder of your week of wisdom.

QUIET TIME REFLECTIONS

Day one: Proverbs 24:1-2, 8-9

1. What word or phrase jumps out to you? Why?

2. Who do you spend most of your time with each week? Is he a positive or negative influence on you? Would God be pleased with that friendship?

3. What's your reputation with those who know you best? Would they say you're wise, or foolish?

Day two: Proverbs 24:3-7

1. What word or phrase jumps out to you? Why?

2. Where do you need wisdom in your life today to be able to stand up under attack or oppression?

3. What wisdom do you have that would be helpful to share with others?

Day three: Proverbs 24:10-12, 15-16

1. What word or phrase jumps out to you? Why?

2. What's a place in your life where you've fallen and need to get back up?

3. Are you acting as a thief toward others in your life in any area? What are you stealing? Joy? Peace? Security? Trust? Hope?

Day four: Proverbs 24:13-14, 26

1. What word or phrase jumps out to you? Why?

2. What's the "best-tasting" wisdom you've ever received? Who did it come from? Would you consider seeking more wisdom from that person?

3. How can you give someone a "kiss" this week? (Figuratively, folks!) Who needs some tender loving care from you?

Day five: Proverbs 24:17-25

1. What word or phrase jumps out to you? Why?

2. Why does the writer have so many "do nots" in these verses? What "do's" do you see?

3. Do you show favoritism toward anyone? How can you be more fair in your judgment and treatment of others?

Day six: Proverbs 24:27-34

1. What word or phrase jumps out to you? Why?

2. Have you witnessed destruction in anyone's life—someone you either know or know about? How could it have been avoided?

3. What might you learn from others' pain and folly?

Day seven: Proverbs 24:1-34

Read through the entire passage. Write down the one verse that impacted you the most this week. Commit the passage to memory.

24. BOXES OF CHOCOLATE
Proverbs 25

LEADER'S INSIGHT

Have you ever received a box of candy as a gift, maybe from your parents, boyfriend, or girlfriend? Did you eat the candy all in one sitting, or did you space it out and enjoy the sweetness for at least a few days? If you chose to spread the candy out a few days, you probably enjoyed it much more than consuming it in a matter of minutes. Too much of a good thing can make you sick.

Most of the Hebrew translations use the word *honey* when talking about sweet foods, as in Proverbs 25:16: "If you find honey, eat just enough—too much of it, and you will vomit." THE MESSAGE version says, "When you're given a box of candy, don't gulp it all down; eat too much chocolate and you'll make yourself sick." Somehow I think chocolate connects more with our culture than honey!

Proverbs 25 tells about the effects of having too much of a good thing. Solomon knew what he was talking about. He chronicled about his own experiences in Ecclesiastes 2:4-5, 7-8:

> I undertook great projects: I built houses for myself and planted vineyards. I made gardens and parks and planted all kinds of fruit trees in them. I also owned more herds and flocks than anyone in Jerusalem before me. I amassed silver and gold for myself, and the treasure of kings and provinces. I acquired male and female singers, and a harem as well—the delights of a man's heart.

Solomon had it all, but how did this leave him feeling about life? "So I hated life, because the work that is done under the sun was grievous to me. All of it is meaningless, a chasing after the wind" (Ecclesiastes 2:17). The wise king gained much wealth and insight in his lifetime.

Help students take this opportunity to learn from the experience of one who had too much. Allow the wisdom of King Solomon to change your life and theirs so you all don't eat too many chocolates.

SHARE

•Have you ever been given a box or bag filled with candy? How did you go about eating it? Did you eat it all at once?

•Is there anything you think you could never have too much of?

•When was the last time you had too much of a good thing? Describe your experience.

OBSERVE

•How many times are similes—using the words *like* or *as* to make a comparison—used in Proverbs 25? What's being compared?

•How many of the similes mentioned above are comparisons to negative things? How many are comparisons to positive things?

•Of what authority figure does Solomon speak most about in this chapter?

•To what kinds of relationships does Solomon make reference?

THINK

- What's the difference between the glory of God and the glory of man (or kings)?

- What's the significance of gold in verses 11 and 12?

- Rewrite verses 16-17 in your own words.

- What are some of the common themes in verses 18-28?

APPLY

- Use a commentary or study Bible to learn more about the meaning of verse 2. What are you discovering? What in your life has God concealed? How are you searching this matter out?

- Read verse 11 in the NIV. If "a word aptly spoken is like apples of gold in settings of silver," which words have you aptly spoken over the last week? In the last six months? The past year?

- Review your list of similes. Which are similar to situations in your life? If you relate to one of the negative similes, how can this situation be improved?

- If you relate to one of the positive similes, explain to everyone how you've grown through the situation.

DO

Pass around a bowl of color-coated chocolate candy. Select a topic for each color (for example, red=worst mistake, blue=greatest victory, green=most embarrassing moment, yellow=a person you would like to meet, etc.) but don't tell the students what each color means. Ask everyone in the circle to grab a handful of five or more pieces of candy. Have each student pick a color from her pile, and you give her the topic to share about based on the color she's chosen. Use this as an activity for the students to get to know one another a little better in a lighthearted manner. Don't play this game too long. We know what happens with too much of a good thing.

QUIET TIME REFLECTIONS

Day one: Proverbs 25:1-3

1. What word or phrase jumps out to you? Why?

2. Use a commentary or study Bible to answer this: Who was Hezekiah?

3. Read Deuteronomy 29:29. How is that verse similar and different from Proverbs 25:2? Go back to your commentary or study Bible. What does it say about verse 3?

Day two: Proverbs 25:4-8

1. What word or phrase jumps out to you? Why?

2. Using a dictionary, find the definition for the word dross. Based on that definition, paraphrase Proverbs 25:5.

3. Read Proverbs 25:6-8. What biblical character found herself in a similar situation? (Hint: Read Esther 4.)

Day three: Proverbs 25:9-14

1. What word or phrase jumps out to you? Why?

2. According to verse 12, which two elements must be present for a rebuke to be seen as an earring or ornament of fine gold?

3. What does a trustworthy messenger do for his senders? How does this apply to your life?

Day four: Proverbs 25:15-17

1. What word or phrase jumps out to you? Why?

2. Read the first half of verse 15. How is this exemplified in the story of Esther you read earlier? (Hint: Read Esther 5:1-8 and Esther 7.)

3. What does it mean to say, "A gentle tongue can break a bone"?

Day five: Proverbs 25:18-20

1. What word or phrase jumps out to you? Why?

2. Have you ever experienced any of the scenarios mentioned in today's verses? Describe your experience.

3. Ask God to help you see what he wants you to see. Ask God if you've ever done to anyone else anything mentioned in these verses. If God shows you that you have, make firm plans to seek forgiveness from others you've wronged during the coming week.

Day six: Proverbs 25:21-28

1. What word or phrase jumps out to you? Why?

2. Have you ever been a blessing to one of your enemies as mentioned in verse 21? If so, please explain. What was your motivation? What happened?

3. According to verse 22, being a blessing to your enemy heaps burning coals on his (or her) head. Does this sound like a good thing to you? Please use a commentary or study Bible to help figure out the meaning of this verse.

Day seven: Proverbs 25:1-28

Read through the entire passage. Write down the one verse that impacted you the most this week. Commit the passage to memory.

25. MAD DOG
Proverbs 26

LEADER'S INSIGHT

The book of Proverbs is sometimes a difficult book to grasp. Many statements are made as though following them would produce black-and-white results, even though they should be considered more as possibilities than promises. It's also difficult to find a specific central truth when so many thoughts fill a single chapter.

In Proverbs 26, Solomon tries to help the readers find his focus more easily by speaking repeatedly of the fool and the sluggard. In Proverbs 26:4-5 Solomon writes, "Do not answer fools according to their folly, or you yourself will be just like them. Answer fools according to their folly, or they will be wise in their own eyes." I read those two verses and say to myself, "So do I answer a fool or not answer a fool? Which is it?" And the answer is: Yes. There's a time to answer a fool and a time not to answer a fool! It's all about wisdom and timing. There's a time to respond in simple terms—there's a time to be quiet.

"As a dog returns to its vomit, so fools repeat their folly. Do you see people who are wise in their own eyes? There is more hope for fools than for them" (Proverbs 26:11-12). The fool gets into quarrels with others: "You grab a mad dog by the ears when you butt into a quarrel that's none of your business" (Proverbs 26:17 MSG). A fool doesn't know when to mind his own business.

Solomon warns the foolish. He also admonishes the lazy person (see Proverbs 26:13-16). In other words, he desires to see the reader grasp the truth and importance of pursuing wisdom and diligence. Those who don't may be likened to fools quoting proverbs, swaying this way and that with little strength to stand firm. (THE MESSAGE says a fool quoting a proverb is "limp as a wet noodle," verse 7.)

As you relate with people, beware of grabbing the mad dog!

SHARE

- Would it be a compliment to be considered a wet noodle? Why or why not?

- When you think of the word *fool,* what comes to mind? *Sluggard?*

- How would you define the word wisdom? Diligence?

OBSERVE

- How many times is the word *fool* used in Proverbs 26?

- To what does Solomon compare a fool?

- How many times is the world *sluggard* used? What do you learn in verses 13-16?

- To what does Solomon compare a sluggard?

THINK

- Why do you think Solomon chooses similes and metaphors to communicate?

- What do you learn about the analogy of dogs in verses 11 and 17? Is there any connection between the two ideas?

- Read verses 4-5. Why do you think those verses are back to back?

- How would you paraphrase verse 22?

APPLY

•Read verses 18-19. Have you ever made light of lying to or deceiving your parents, brothers, sisters, or friends? What do you need to do this week to begin to seek their forgiveness and to begin restoring their trust in you?

•Read verse 28. According to this verse, lying and flattery both bring destruction. What will you do this week to guard your words so they don't bring destruction?

•Which verse did you relate to most? Was it for negative or positive reasons?

•Commit to memorizing a passage that spoke to you most this week, asking God to help you become all he created you to be.

DO

Play the old game "Telephone." Have everyone sit in a circle. Select one person (who becomes the leader) to think of a phrase to be whispered in the ear of the person to his left. Once the leader whispers the phrase into the ear of the person to his left, that person then whispers the same phrase (or what they heard of it) into the person's ear on her left. This continues until the last person in the circle has heard the phrase. No one can repeat the phrase, and the last person to hear must say what he heard (or thinks he heard) out loud. It's always interesting to hear how the original phrase has changed. Share with students how this activity shows what happens when communication gets out of control, much like when people gossip and speak foolishly.

QUIET TIME REFLECTIONS

Day one: Proverbs 26:1-3

1. What word or phrase jumps out to you? Why?

2. Why do you think that "honor is not fitting for a fool"?

3. Use a study Bible or commentary to better understand verse 2. Take time to paraphrase this verse. What do halters do for donkeys? What do whips do for horses? What then should a rod do for a fool?

Day two: Proverbs 26:4-5

1. What word or phrase jumps out to you? Why?

2. Give an example of how answering a fool according to her foolishness will make you become like her.

3. Give an example of how answering a fool according to his foolishness can keep him from being wise in his own eyes.

Day three: Proverbs 26:6-10

1. What word or phrase jumps out to you? Why?

2. What do you think Solomon means by the term fool? Feel free to use Bible study resources to find your answer.

3. Read verses 6-10 in the NIV. Why does Solomon use "cutting off one's feet" and "drinking violence" in the same proverb? What then does it mean to "send a message by the hand of a fool"? Spend time analyzing and understanding the metaphors in verses 7-10.

Day four: Proverbs 26:11-20

1. What word or phrase jumps out to you? Why?

2. Why do you think a fool has more hope than someone who's wise in her own eyes (verse 12)?

3. According to verse 20, what's one reason to keep away from gossip?

Day five: Proverbs 26:21-22

1. What word or phrase jumps out to you? Why?

2. Explain the comparison of charcoal to embers and wood to a fire. Now take time to explain the relationship of quarreling to an argument ("kindling strife").

3. What are choice morsels? Use any resources you need to find the answer. How do you think words of gossip going to a person's innermost parts affect the person?

Day six: Proverbs 26:23-28

1. What word or phrase jumps out to you? Why?

2. What are three ways a malicious person can disguise herself?

3. According to verses 24-26 what are some characteristics of a malicious person? Spend some time thinking and praying over verse 28. How has this verse proven true in your life?

Day seven: Proverbs 26:1-28

Read through the entire passage. Write down the one verse that impacted you the most this week. Commit the passage to memory.

26. KNOW YOUR CONDITION
Proverbs 27

LEADER'S INSIGHT

Life can be hard. We have opportunity after opportunity to choose right from wrong, to glorify God with everything we do and say. Living a life glorifying to God isn't easy. We're all in need of friends and family who can remind us to choose joy on a daily basis.

Proverbs 27 is about knowing our condition—assessing where our hearts are and where they aren't. Some of the principles in this chapter are—don't brag about the future because we have no idea where it will take us (1); we're not to praise ourselves, rather we are to let others do it (2); be careful with anger (4); don't talk loudly to a neighbor in the morning (14); and resist being a quarrelsome person, likened to the "dripping of a leaky roof in a rainstorm" (15).

Solomon has some great wisdom about how we should think of ourselves and treat those around us so we don't end up in dangerous situations. Solomon teaches about love and friendships and how they can protect us. Proverbs 27:5-6 says, "Better is open rebuke than hidden love. Wounds from a friend can be trusted, but an enemy multiplies kisses." The great power and influence in relationships make us who we are. Solomon writes, "As iron sharpens iron, so one person sharpens another. As water reflects the face, so one's life reflects the heart" (Proverbs 27:17, 19).

As you study this chapter, look for God to speak truth into your life. My hope is when the week is done, you and your students will have found wisdom and strength for the journey ahead—and in the process discovered more about the condition of your lives.

SHARE

•Give an example of a friend who helps you be a better person.

•Tell of a time you knew you shouldn't do something and you did it anyway.

•Why do you think it's important to have friends and know your neighbors?

OBSERVE

•How many times does this chapter use the word *friend?*

•What does the writer compare a quarrelsome wife to in Proverbs 27:15-16?

•What does verse 21 say people are tested by? What does verse 2 say about how a person should get praise?

•What does verse 8 compare to a person who strays from his home?

THINK

•Look at verse 14. Why do you think this early morning blessing would be taken as a curse?

•What do you think it means to sharpen someone like iron (verse 17)?

•What do you think it means when verse 24 says, "Riches do not endure forever, and a crown is not secure for all generations"?

•What warning do you think verse 1 is giving, and why do you think this is important?

APPLY

•Verse 5 talks about an open rebuke being better than hidden love. Is there someone in your life you're giving hidden love to? Why do you think an open rebuke would be better than this kind of love?

•Do you have people in your life who aren't sincere friends, but build you up for the wrong reasons (as in verse 6)? Are there people in your life who treat you with kisses but really carry contempt for (look down on) you?

•Look at verse 3. How do you need to work harder at not provoking others (friends, siblings, parents, acquaintances)?

•Verse 4 describes how jealousy and anger are similar and different. Can you think of some times your jealousy might have hurt someone else? Hurt yourself? What are some ways you can work on your struggle with jealousy?

DO

Create a jealousy and anger meter. Write these words on the top of a sheet for each student in your group to copy onto a piece of paper:

THE JEALOUSY AND ANGER METER

|—————————————————————————————————————|

not at all   sometimes   most of the time

During the week have your students journal, describing every time they get angry or jealous. By the end of the week, have them circle which of the three responses fit them the most: Not at all, sometimes, or most of time. Have them share their insights with your group next week.

QUIET TIME REFLECTIONS

Day one: Proverbs 27:1-5

1. What word or phrase jumps out to you? Why?

2. Which one of these proverbs do you need to work on the most?

3. What could you do to improve in that area of your life?

Day two: Proverbs 27:6-10

1. What word or phrase jumps out to you? Why?

2. Do you think you're a good friend to others? Do you have quality friends you can depend on for advice, help, and even correction once in a while?

3. If you don't have these kinds of friends, where might you be able to seek out friends like this?

Day three: Proverbs 27:11-14

1. What word or phrase jumps out to you? Why?

2. Would you consider yourself wise? Do you feel like you bring joy to your parents' hearts?

3. In what ways can you work on being wiser and more prudent when you see danger and making life easier on your parents and yourself?

Day four: Proverbs 27:15-20

1. What word or phrase jumps out to you? Why?

2. Does anyone in your life sharpen you? Do you sharpen anyone?

3. Think about someone who needs you to be fully present with him. Spend time listening and encouraging him today. Describe your experience.

Day five: Proverbs 27:21-23

1. What word or phrase jumps out to you? Why?

2. What does it mean that "people are tested by their praise"?

3. Why do you want or need praise from certain people?

Day six: Proverbs 27:24-27

1. What word or phrase jumps out to you? Why?

2. What does this phrase mean: "The lambs will provide you with clothing"?

3. Spend some time today thinking about how your life is comfortable compared to the way most of the world lives. Jot down some of your ideas.

Day seven: Proverbs 27:1-27

Read through the entire passage. Write down the one verse that impacted you the most this week. Commit the passage to memory.

27. PLAYING FAVORITES?
Proverbs 28

LEADER'S INSIGHT

Whether it was for kick the can, dodgeball, or tag football, we learned as kids to always pick the best and most popular kids first and the worst and "least likely to succeed" last. It was always a tense moment when the last two kids stood together. To make matters worse, often it was one boy and one girl. If the girl got picked, the boy was humiliated. If the girl was picked last, she thought her gender was less than best. Nobody won. (I was chosen last behind the girl many times... wherever you are, I forgive you.)

Proverbs 28 addresses playing favorites. THE MESSAGE says, "Playing favorites is always a bad thing; you can do great harm in seemingly harmless ways" (21). God doesn't like favoritism. Proverbs describes God's disdain when a ruler oppresses the poor (3), when the rich have perverse ways (6), and when people pray but don't listen (9).

Why is playing favorites so dangerous and humiliating at times? "To show partiality is not good—yet a person will do wrong for a piece of bread" (Proverbs 28:21). That's what your students will explore in this session about playing favorites.

SHARE

- Can you name a time when you were picked last or told you couldn't play in a game?

- What's it like to be ignored by someone? How does it make you feel?

- Why do we choose some people to hang out with and leave others behind?

OBSERVE

- Read Proverbs 28:1-7. What's one of the major themes of this passage?

- What do verses 8-14 have to say about money and materialism?

- Look at verses 15-21. Which verses deal with favoritism?

- Verses 22-28 describe a generous heart and a greedy person. What insights do you gain from these passages?

THINK

- Based on verses 1-5, what kind of leadership do we need and not need in government?

- Why do you think justice (verse 5) is a central theme in Proverbs? What does God have to do with justice issues?

- Why do you think we conceal our sins (verses 9, 13), and how does this affect our relationship with God?

- Why does verse 26 suggest trusting in yourself makes you a fool? How is this different from self-confidence?

APPLY

- Have you ever experienced being left out of a group? If yes, how did it feel?

- What feels more painful, to exclude someone or to be excluded? Why?

- What's the difference, besides money, between what the Bible calls the rich and the poor? Which are you? Explain.

- What do you think verse 27 wants us to consider doing in a response to the poor?

DO

Go to a park and have your students take some time for solitude and reflection. Ask each member of the group to think of one or two names of people they consider poor, uncool, unpopular, loners, or losers—whatever phrases you want students to consider. As they walk around the park by themselves, ask them to pray about finding ways of being inclusive, not exclusive with the people they named—and then have them try out any insights they received over the next week. Have each student report back next week about how it went.

QUIET TIME REFLECTIONS

Day one: Proverbs 28:1-4

1. What word or phrase jumps out to you? Why?

2. What do you think it means to be a person of "understanding and knowledge"?

3. Spend some time today praying to know God more intimately and deeply.

Day two: Proverbs 28:5-9

1. What word or phrase jumps out to you? Why?

2. What do you think this means: "Companions of gluttons disgrace their parents"?

3. Spend some time today thinking about ways to bring honor and not disgrace to your mom or dad. Write down your ideas.

Day three: Proverbs 28:10-15

1. What word or phrase jumps out to you? Why?

2. What promises are given in these verses? How can we obtain them?

3. How can you experience all God has for you?

Day four: Proverbs 28:16-20

1. What word or phrase jumps out to you? Why?

2. Why do you think it says those who "chase fantasies will have their fill of poverty"?

3. What selfish fantasies do you have? What God-given dreams keep you up at night?

Day five: Proverbs 28:21-24

1. What word or phrase jumps out to you? Why?

2. How does favoritism ruin people?

3. In what ways do you include or exclude others?

Day six: Proverbs 28:25-28

1. What word or phrase jumps out to you? Why?

2. Why does God stress the value of helping the poor?

3. What can you do to minister to the poor?

Day seven: Proverbs 28:1-28

Read through the entire passage. Write down the one verse that impacted you the most this week. Commit the passage to memory.

28. CYNICS OR SAGES?
Proverbs 29

LEADER'S INSIGHT

The President of the United States: Every four years we start the political process of searching for a presidential candidate. It can be a long and arduous journey for those desiring to lead the United States. They usually endure a lot of verbal mudslinging and character attacks. In the process it's easy for us to get cynical about leadership.

Proverbs 29 deals with the hard reality of leadership. Proverbs 29:2 says, "When good people run things, everyone is glad, but when the ruler is bad, everyone groans" (MSG). The TNIV says, "When the righteous thrive, the people rejoice; when the wicked rule, the people groan."

Webster's Dictionary defines a cynic as "a fault-finding, captious critic, especially one who believes that human conduct is motivated wholly by self-interest." Unfortunately, students can pick up this attribute pretty quickly from us adults! Proverbs 29:8 says, "A gang of cynics can upset a whole city; a group of sages can calm everyone down" (MSG). Proverbs call leaders sages in the next verse as well: "A sage trying to work things out with a fool gets only scorn and sarcasm for his trouble" (29:9 MSG).

What is a sage? Webster's defines a sage as "a profound philosopher distinguished for wisdom" and "a mature or venerable man of sound judgment." In this chapter we'll discover the sage knows how to handle anger, how to trust God during hard times, and how to be a vision caster—and a sage fears God over people.

Your students are at ages and stages when they need to consider being mentored and mentoring others. Some of your students are emerging sages with dreams, goals, and visions to make a difference. We have to find ways to unleash them, empowering them to be the godly leaders of the future. The question is: Do we have cynics or sages?

SHARE

- If you could spend time with any leader from the past or present, who would that be and why?

- Name some leaders in today's world. What qualities make them leaders?

- If you could add one leadership trait to your life, what would it be, and how would you use it?

OBSERVE

- What principles does Proverbs 29:1-6 mention for leadership?

- Read verses 7-14. What traits mentioned in this passage could bring down a good leader?

- Verse 18 mentions that a leader needs revelation or vision. If a leader has no direction or vision, what's the result?

- What happens when we fear people over God, according to verse 25?

THINK

- Why do you think some people make the same mistakes over and over and seem unteachable (verses 1-2)?

- From verse 13, what do you think it means that "God gives sight to the eyes of both oppressor and the poor"?

•From verse 15, what does this mean: "Children left to themselves disgrace their mother"?

•How does verse 16 tell us to deal with wicked leadership and abusive power?

APPLY

•Has God ever given you a revelation or dream? What was it? Has it become reality?

•What do you think it means to be a person who speaks in haste? Is this a compliment or a criticism?

•Have you ever been so angry you caused a stir? What happened? How would you respond differently now?

•Has God ever humbled you through a difficult experience? What do you think was God trying to teach you?

DO

Either beforehand or together with students during your meeting time, come up with a long list of all of the leaders you can think of from Hitler (bad) to Jesus (good). List 20-30 names, even names of people you know. Next to each name, list one trait that makes the person a leader. Following that list, add the name of each member of your group. Then ask other group members to write one trait of leadership next to someone else's name.

QUIET TIME REFLECTIONS

Day one: Proverbs 29:1-3

1. What word or phrase jumps out to you? Why?

2. Why do you think this passage uses the word *stiff-necked?* What does it mean?

3. How can you remain teachable to God's ways?

Day two: Proverbs 29:4-7

1. What word or phrase jumps out to you? Why?

2. What does this passage state about anger, jealousy, and flattery?

3. How might you avoid conflict with others?

Day three: Proverbs 29:8-12

1. What word or phrase jumps out to you? Why?

2. What do we learn about handling rage and anger?

3. What do you usually do with your anger?

Day four: Proverbs 29:13-18

1. What word or phrase jumps out to you? Why?

2. What do we learn about discipline with parents and children?

3. In what ways can you learn from your parents' discipline?

Day five: Proverbs 29:19-23

1. What word or phrase jumps out to you? Why?

2. What does this passage say about hot-tempered people?

3. Spend some time today thinking about the right ways to handle conflict. List some ideas.

Day six: Proverbs 29:24-27

1. What word or phrase jumps out to you? Why?

2. What are the righteous and wicked battling over?

3. How do people in our society "seek an audience"? How do you sometimes do this?

Day seven: Proverbs 29:1-27

Read through the entire passage. Write down the one verse that impacted you the most this week. Commit the passage to memory.

[From *Studies on the Go: The Book of Proverbs* by Dr. David Olshine. Permission granted to reproduce this page for use in buyer's youth group. Copyright ©2009 by Youth Specialties.]

29. REPETITION
Proverbs 30

LEADER'S INSIGHT

4x5=20. True, but this isn't the equation in Proverbs 30. Agur, possibly a descendant of Ishmael (the half-brother of Isaac), a non-Israelite from North Arabia, begins Proverbs 30 by assuming two different personalities. First he speaks as the arrogant person who doesn't believe in God and second as the humble follower of God who stakes his or her life on God's every word. Which one are you?

In the first four verses Agur raises a frustration almost any follower of God will experience at some point—the absence of God. What Agur is wrestling with is that with all of our human knowledge and wisdom, God still seems elusive and somewhat hidden. That's because God is bigger than our finite minds can handle. Agur asks, "Who has gone up to heaven and come down? Whose hands have gathered up the wind? Who has wrapped up the waters in a cloak? Who has established all the ends of the earth?" (Proverbs 30:4) Agur later seems to decide God is BIG and mysterious, and if we could figure everything all out, then we would be God.

In verses 5-6 Agur helps ease the pain of not fully being able to understand God by telling us we have God's Word, which is "flawless; he is a shield to those who take refuge in him." God can be experienced and known on planet Earth.

Agur continues and completes Proverbs 30 by mentioning five different categories each containing four elements, objects, or examples. Repetition always meant something to the Hebrew people. Repetition means God is saying something worth repeating, hearing, and then applying in our lives. We should pay attention to the repeating style to understand fully what Agur is trying to tell us about God.

SHARE

•What's your favorite school subject? Why?

•What word or phrase do you repeat most often in a day?

•If you could spend the rest of your days communicating one life-changing truth to others, what would it be? How would you do it?

OBSERVE

•Who wrote Proverbs 30? List everything you learn about him from verse 1.

•What five actions does Agur caution his reader against in verses 10-14?

•Give a title to each of the five different categories Agur lists.

•Under each category title list the four elements or objects Agur gives as examples of each category.

THINK

•Why do you think Agur chose to write about the two contrasting personalities in verses 2-4 and verses 5-6?

•Proverbs 30:7-9 is the only prayer in the book of Proverbs. What do you think is the purpose of the prayer found here?

•Agur's prayer (mentioned above) asks for two different types of things. What are they?

•Paraphrase verses 32-33. Why do you think Agur uses these two verses to wrap up this chapter?

APPLY

•Would you say verses 3-4 or verses 5-6 describe your life? Please explain your answer.

•Which of the five don'ts in verses 10-14 do you struggle with most? How will you handle that struggle this week?

•When was the last time you were disrespectful of your parents or those you live with? Spend time as a group writing letters to your parents, asking their forgiveness for some of these things.

•Read verse 32. Have you ever played the fool, exalted yourself, or planned evil? Did it work for you? What was the result of your actions?

DO

In chapter 30 of Proverbs, Agur uses lists. For this activity your group will spend time making a list of encouraging words for each person in the group. First, grab a blank sheet of notebook paper for each person present. Pass out the papers and have each person write his or her name on the top of the page. Then everyone should number from 1-20 down the left side of the paper. Next, pass the papers around so every person in the group gets the opportunity to write at least one encouraging word or phrase about the person whose name is at the top of the list. Continue passing the papers around until everyone has 20 encouraging words or phrases on his or her own piece of paper. Spend some time discussing what's listed under each person's name. Ask some questions like, What surprises you about what's written under your name? What makes you smile? How has this activity encouraged you?

QUIET TIME REFLECTIONS

Day one: Proverbs 30:1-9

1. What word or phrase jumps out to you? Why?

2. List the characteristics of the proud person in verses 2-4. List the characteristics of the humble person in verses 5-6.

3. Spend time reading and rereading Agur's prayer (verses 7-9). What stands out to you?

Day two: Proverbs 30:10-14

1. What word or phrase jumps out to you? Why?

2. If you had to name the sins listed in these verses, what would you say they are?

3. Read 2 Timothy 3:1-7. How do these New Testament verses in 2 Timothy parallel these Old Testament verses in Proverbs?

Day three: Proverbs 30:15-20

1. What word or phrase jumps out to you? Why?

2. What four things are never satisfied or never say enough? Why do they leave us unsatisfied?

3. What four things are amazing and incomprehensible? Why?

Day four: Proverbs 30:21-28

1. What word or phrase jumps out to you? Why?

2. What four things cause the earth to tremble? How so?

3. What four things are small and wise? What makes them so?

Day five: Proverbs 30:29-31

1. What word or phrase jumps out to you? Why?

2. What four things have an amazing stride? What makes them so amazing?

3. Use a study Bible or Bible commentary to discover why Agur consistently says three...(then) four. What's the reason?

Day six: Proverbs 30:32-33

1. What word or phrase jumps out to you? Why?

2. What should you do if you find yourself being foolish, being arrogant, or plotting evil?

3. What can we know will happen for sure if someone churns milk, punches someone in the nose, or agitates an already angry person?

Day seven: Proverbs 30:1-33

Read through the entire passage. Write down the one verse that impacted you the most this week. Commit the passage to memory.

30. KEEP FOCUSED
Proverbs 31

LEADER'S INSIGHT

In Proverbs 31:1-9, the king is being reminded to guard himself from distractions that would keep him from fulfilling the highest and most important goals of his kingship: Helping those who can't help themselves and protecting those who are oppressed. I appreciate the fact that the king needs a reminder not to get distracted. This means he isn't all together, and if he isn't careful, he could find himself being distracted by other things.

As we look at the second half of this chapter of Proverbs, notice that the godly woman being described keeps her most important goals of being a wife and mother at the forefront. She is careful not to get distracted by the many other things in life that could prevent her from fulfilling her goals. She's of noble character (Proverbs 31:10), her husband trusts her, and she's an entrepreneur in the home (13-19). She's a caring woman who "opens her arms to the poor and extends her hands to the needy"(20). She's a domestic engineer and makes sure the needs of the house and her family are taken care of, watching "over the affairs of the household" (27), and her children respect and love her. What makes her so special? "A woman who fears the Lord is to be praised" (30).

As Christians, whether we're students, sons, daughters, mothers, or fathers, we must not get distracted from the purpose and goals God has for each of us at the places where we're at in our lives.

In the story of Mary and Martha in Luke 10:38-42, Jesus told Martha, who was scurrying around, trying to prepare a meal for him, "Martha, Martha, you are worried and upset about many things, but few things are needed—or indeed only one. Mary has chosen what is better." Mary learned to resist distractions and focus on being in the presence of God. Proverbs 31 will help us see how to live this way.

SHARE

- Can you think of anyone you would call a woman of noble character?

- What are some life goals you need to focus on?

- What are some distractions you need to be aware of in your own life?

OBSERVE

- What are the distractions in Proverbs 31:1-9 that the king's mom tells him to be aware of?

- Look at verses 11 and 28. What do these say this woman's husband and children think of her?

- Read verses 10-31 and write down all the things this woman spends her time doing. What are some characteristics these verses say she has?

- In verse 23, what do we learn about this woman's husband?

THINK

- Look up the word *noble*. From the definition, what about this woman do you think exemplifies this word's meaning?

- In verses 21-22, the writer mentions the colors scarlet and purple for this wife and her children's clothes and says the garments are made of linen. What do you think these colors and fabrics symbolize? Why do you think it would be important to mention the colors and type of material?

•In verse 30 what does the author say about beauty and charm? What does the author say is important? Why do you think the author stresses the deception and fleetingness of charm and beauty?

•Why do you think in the midst of talking about this woman's noble character, the author places verse 23 in the middle where it talks about the type of husband she has?

APPLY

•After looking at verses 3-7, can you think of some distractions keeping you from fulfilling the goals God has for you right now?

•Reread verses 11 and 28. What do you think the people closest to you would say about you? If you aren't happy with the answer you get, what can you do to improve how people perceive you?

•Look at verse 26. Wisdom and faithful instruction come from the woman's mouth. Do you feel people would say you speak words of wisdom and faithful instruction? If no, how do you think you can work on this?

•Read verse 23. When looking for people to date or marry, what are you looking for? Are you looking only at people who are respected by their community, family, and friends? One who is trusted in leadership? If not, why do you think you're settling for someone who is less than the person described here?

DO

Have the group rewrite a contemporary story of a Proverbs 31 woman. They can create a profile of a mother and wife, a single professional woman, or a teenage girl. The service and activities of these types of women may be different, but the personal characteristics should still be the same.

QUIET TIME REFLECTIONS

Day one: Proverbs 31:1-9

1. What word or phrase jumps out to you? Why?

2. Do you struggle with any of these distractions?

3. What could you do to improve in that area of your life?

Day two: Proverbs 31:10-15

1. What word or phrase jumps out to you? Why?

2. What is this woman doing in these verses that's so important?

3. How might you help provide for those around you? How could you begin doing this?

Day three: Proverbs 31:16-19

1. What word or phrase jumps out to you? Why?

2. This woman makes sure her time, money, and energy are well-spent. Do you feel you're conscientious about how you spend your time, energy, and money?

3. What are some ways you can improve how you spend your time, energy, and money?

Day four: Proverbs 31:20-23

1. What word or phrase jumps out to you? Why?

2. In what ways do you open your arms to the poor and extend your hands to the needy?

3. What are some qualities in this text you want in a future spouse?

Day five: Proverbs 31:24-27

1. What word or phrase jumps out to you? Why?

2. What do you think verse 25 means when it says, "She can laugh at the days to come"?

3. Think about some characteristics people would say about you when it comes to how you speak, work, or use your time. What would you like others to say?

Day six: Proverbs 31:28-31

1. What word or phrase jumps out to you? Why?

2. What would your parents and friends say about you? Are you happy with what you think their responses would be? If not, what do you need to do to work on this?

3. Do you feel you sometimes depend on your charm and beauty rather than fearing God? If so, in what ways can you begin to depend more on God?

Day seven: Proverbs 31:1-31

Read through the entire passage. Write down the one verse that impacted you the most this week. Commit the passage to memory.

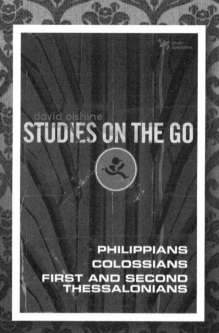

Written with the busy youth worker in mind, books in the Studies on the Go series will provide Scriptural depth and substance to be tackled in a manageable timeframe. The questions are real and get straight to the point. As students study Philippians, Colossians, and First and Second Thessalonians, they will learn how to find joy in their journey, discover practical instructions of faith, and get encouragement for times of trial.

Studies on the Go: Philippians, Colossians, First and Second Thessalonians

David Olshine
Retail $8.99
978-0-310-28549-6

Visit www.youthspecialties.com
or your local bookstore.

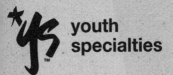

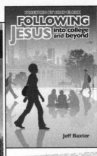

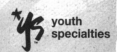

YOUTH SPECIALTIES

Studies on the Go: Proverbs
Copyright 2009 by David Olshine

Youth Specialties resources, 1890 Cordell Ct. Ste. 105, El Cajon, CA 92020 are published by Zondervan, 5300 Patterson Ave. SE, Grand Rapids, MI 49530.

Library of Congress Cataloging-in-Publication Data

Olshine, David, 1954-
Proverbs / by David Olshine.
    p. cm. — (Studies on the go)
ISBN 978-0-310-28548-9 (soft cover)
1. Bible. O.T. Proverbs—Study and teaching. I. Title.
BS1467.O47 2009
223'.707—dc22   2009009968

Cover design by Toolbox Studios
Interior design by SharpSeven Design

Printed in the United States of America

11 12 13 14 • 20 19 18 17 16 15 14 13 12 11 10 9 8 7 6 5 4

david olshine

STUDIES ON THE GO

PROVERBS

ZONDERVAN.com/
AUTHORTRACKER
follow your favorite authors